DARK PSYCHOLOGY AND MANIPULATION:

THE ULTIMATE GUIDE TO LEARN THE ART OF PERSUASION. DISCOVER SECRET METHODS FOR INFLUENCE PEOPLE, MIND CONTROL AND HYPNOSIS. DEFEND YOURSELF FROM NARCISSISTIC ABUSE.

PAUL CARTER

Dark Psychology

Introduction

It is not uncommon for humans to make attempts at influencing others by making use of psychological techniques such as manipulation, coercion, persuasion, deception, hypnosis, mind games and brainwashing.

Psychology is the study of the mental process of humans. It seeks to investigate the thought process of humans by looking critically at the reason why people do what they do and the way they do it.

When it comes to dark psychology, the focus is on the human condition in relation to the nature of the psyche of humans, which propels them to prey on other people with the aim of influencing them. This is driven by criminal or deviant tendencies which lack purpose, as well as other general assumptions of both social science and instinctual drives.

All the members of humanity have the tendency to victimize other people, as well as every living creature on Earth. For some people, these tendencies are restrained and very minimal, while others easily fall for the instinct and act upon these impulses.

Typically, what dark psychology strives to achieve is the understanding of the thoughts, feelings and perceptions that lead to the predatory behavior of a human being. However, it assumes that the production of this feeling and quest to influence others has a purpose and some rational, goal-oriented motivation about 99 percent of the time. The remaining 1 percent falls under dark psychology, characterized by a brutal victimization of other people with an intent devoid of purpose or a logical definition with either evolutionary science or religious dogma.

According to dark psychology, every human has a bank of malevolent intentions geared towards other people and these intentions range from fleeting thoughts to minimally obtrusiveness to pure psychopathic deviant characters that are devoid of any form of cohesive rationality. This is described with a term known as the Dark Continuum.

Also, there is another term known as the Dark Factor, which refers to the mitigating factors that act as accelerants or attractive factors to every form of approaching Dark Singularity, which indicates the point where a person's heinous actions fall in the radar of the Dark Continuum.

Michael Nuccitelli (2006) states that dark psychology isn't only the dark side of the moon, but the dark side of the combination of all the moons. It is a combination of everything that makes an individual who they are in relation to their dark sides. It is a trait that is present in every religion, culture, faith, as well as every race of humanity.

From the point of birth to the point of death, there is an inherent not-so-pleasant side within everyone, which some have described as evil, while others call it deviant, criminal and/or pathological.

With dark psychology, there is an introduction of a third philosophical construct, which looks at these behaviors from a different angle aside from religious dogmas and contemporary theories of social science. To be successful, every individual must take an interest in their fellow humanity. It is from the lack of interest in others that every failure in life springs and this causes great injury to others. All human failures arise from this type of individuals (Alfred Adler, n.d.).

According to the tenets of dark psychology, some of those who commit these acts do not do so for the love of money, power, sex, retribution or any other known motivation. They just merely commit these horrid acts without any goal at all. They easily simplify their ends and do not justify their means.

Some other people just violate or cause injury to other people for the sake of doing so and the potential for this lies within the core of everyone—a drive to harm other people without any reason, explanation or purpose.

According to dark psychology, this is a complex potential that is hard to define. It states that the potential to become a predator, which is present in everyone, has access to people's thoughts, feelings and even their perceptions. The good thing is that it is only few people that act on this potential.

At one point or the other, every human will have had thoughts or feeling of acting towards another person in a brutal manner and many times would have had thoughts or the feelings of hurting someone else without mercy. To be honest with oneself is to accept the fact that at a certain point in time, there has been a feeling of wanting to commit some heinous acts.

As a result of the fact that humans consider themselves to be a benevolent species, it isn't surprising that most times humans want to believe and convince themselves that these thoughts and feelings are non-existent, but the truth is that these thoughts are always present in everyone.

In dark psychology, it is believed that this predatorial side of human nature is of a certain purpose. Several fields of religion, psychology and other dogmas have attempted to give a solid definition to dark psychology.

Although it is true that most areas of human behavior related to evil actions have a purpose and a goal, when it comes to dark psychology, the aspect that is concerned with goal oriented and purposive motivation seems to become very indistinct.

There exists a continuum of dark psychology victimization which ranges from thoughts and spans all the way to pure psychopathic deviance. However, this contributes to helping in conceptualizing the philosophy of dark psychology.

The aspect of the human psyche which dark psychology addresses, is that which makes room for these predatory behaviors. In many cases, these behavioral tendencies are characterized by a lack of obvious rational motivation which is universal and lacks predictability.

In dark psychology, it is assumed that the universal human condition is quite different, or it can be said to be an extension of human evolution. However, to give a critical look at this concept it is important to study the tenets of evolution. This means that one will first consider that the evolution of man started from the life of other animals and now man has become the paragon of all other animal life.

This is thanks to the frontal lobes of the brain which make room for the human to be the apex creature. Therefore, it is valid to assume the fact that man as the apex creature does not make him completely isolated from both his animal instincts and his predatory nature.

If there is any truth in this evolutionary theory, and if you belong to the league of those who believe in the theory, you will agree with the fact that every behavior has something to do with three instincts: aggression, sex and self-sustenance. These are the primary instincts that drive humans.

In the evolutionary theory, there is a tenet of the survival of the fittest which is replicated in other species. In other to survive and reproduce, there is a similarity between humans and all other life forms. To be able to mark one's territory, there must be a show of aggression. This also goes a long way in protecting these marked territories, as well as gaining the right to procreate.

Although this may seem to be a rational process of thoughts and action, it is not a part of the human condition in the purest sense of it. Therefore, it is important to note that dark psychology is not applicable when it comes to other animals on the planet, as it is only humans that are prone to exhibiting the tenets of dark psychology. However, a critical look at the human condition will dissolve the theories of natural selection, evolution and animal instincts as humans are the only species that are able to prey on themselves without any apparent reason of procreation in order to survive and sustain humanity.

Humans prey on one another for reasons that are not clear and cannot be sustained. It is this part of the human mental state or what is known as the universal human condition, that dark psychology aims at addressing; the part that makes humans impel this predatory attitude.

In dark psychology, it is believed that there is an intrapsychic part of human nature that makes people do what they do in terms of preying on others and this part of human nature goes against the tenets of evolution. Humans are also the only other creatures on the planet that will kill one another for reasons other than the want of food, survival, territory or procreation.

For ages, philosophers and other ecclesiastical writers have made several attempts at looking at this phenomenon in order to explain it. What has only been discovered is the fact that it is only human beings that harm themselves without any form of rational motivation.

It is assumed in dark psychology that there is a part of the human psyche that gives life to these dark and vicious characters and this part within all human beings is universal. At this point, in the past or in the future, there hasn't been any human creature that did not possess this dark side.

Chapter 1.Delving into Dark Psychology

Theoretical Overview

The work of Dr. Nuccitelli is based upon work completed by Dr. Alfred Adler. At the beginning of the 20th century, Dr. Adler, a medical doctor, psychologist, philosopher, and contemporary of Dr. Carl Jung and Dr. Sigmund Freud, compiled a volume of work exploring many behavioral and psychological theories in an effort to explain why some people are prone to commit acts of predatory violence and abuse. From the perspective of Dr. Adler, all human behavior is motivated by a rational purpose. Thus, for Adler, neither good behavior nor bad behavior can be attributed to the basic, fundamental character of the person; instead, all behavior can only be explained by examining the motivations and goals of the person.

For example, a benevolent or kind person behaves in such a manner, not because he or she is a fundamentally kind or caring person, but because he or she has been taught since childhood that kind, caring, and contributory behavior is more likely to result in acceptance by social groups. Further, acceptance into social groups is often an indicator of the likelihood of success in other areas of life.

Similarly, Adler regarded all hostile and predatory behavior as also the result of deliberate purpose and intent. According to Adler, people who commit acts of violence, aggression, or other forms of predation and violation are responding to a deep sense of inferiority. Rejection by a social group can cause the subject of rejection to develop a tendency to move in a negative direction that can lead to further isolation, thereby creating a progressive tendency to develop behavior that is unkind, disrespectful, or otherwise undignified.

Adler, Freud, and Jung all subscribed to the philosophy of teleology, which states that all entities have an end function, goal, or purpose. Under this philosophical construct, all human behavior—good, bad, or otherwise—must be regarded as purposive (i.e., serving some practical purpose). As a result, all human behavior, no matter how deviant, can eventually be understood by examining the practical motives of the actor.

Dr. Nuccitelli has been influential in developing the theories of dark psychology. These theories regard the work of Dr. Adler as extremely important. Dark psychology theory agrees that 99.99% of all human behavior is purposive and can be explained through rational means. However, Nuccitelli differs by insisting that that there is .01% of human psychology that is capable of developing harmful and destructive behavior that serves no knowable practical purpose whatsoever. This capacity is what is meant by dark psychology.

There are some important terms that will help readers understand the language of dark psychology, including Dark Continuum, Dark Factor, Dark Singularity. Because this limits its focus specifically to problems caused by emotional predators and emotional manipulation, we will examine only these three terms.

Dark Continuum: Imagine the Dark Continuum as a line used to gauge the nature and severity of behavior based in dark psychology. Mild and purposive acts fall to the left of the continuum, while severe and purposeless acts fall to the right.

For example, if we use the Dark Continuum to measure the types of conduct that exhibit traits of dark psychology, then psychological and emotional violations would tend to appear on the left side of the continuum, while acts of physical violence would appear on the right side of the continuum.

Of course, an extremely severe emotional or psychological violation committed for purely sadistic purposes may appear further to the right on the continuum than a less severe act of physical violence committed for a rational purpose.

Dark Factor. The Dark Factor is a term used to describe the latent, inherent capacity of all human beings to act with malevolence. This term expresses a theoretical concept to explain the human propensity to develop personality traits that lead to the likelihood that someone will engage in acts of willful violence, destruction, or harm to others.

There are many influences that may exacerbate or lessen the chance that the latent capacity for abuse will be activated. However, all people possess a Dark Factor in their psychological makeup.

Dark Singularity. This term is also used to describe a theoretical concept. It borrows from the language of physics, which describes a singularity as the absolute center of a black hole. The singularity at the center of a black hole contains energy and gravity that is so dense and powerful that, as objects approach it, they became ensnared in its gravitational pull to the point that they cannot escape. Even light can become trapped in the singularity of a black hole.

To gain a better understanding of dark psychology, Dr. Nuccitelli has compiled the following six tenets that define the nature and function of dark psychology:

1. All people possess the capacity for dark psychology. Dark psychology is not a genetic defect or flaw, but a universal aspect of the human condition.

2. Dark psychology studies the innate human potential for developing predatory behavior that does not serve any practical purpose. Thus, if 99.99% of human behavior is designed to achieve a practical goal, dark psychology represents that .01% capacity within human psychology to engage in conduct with an end-goal of causing pain, harm, and damage.

3. Dark psychology seeks to fill gaps in the explanation of destructive and harmful human behavior and takes the position that dark psychological behavior traits can manifest themselves anywhere on a continuum of predatory behavior, from mild deviance to extreme violence.

4. The Dark Continuum is not defined exclusively by the end act of deviance or violence, but by the practical, psychological motivations of the person. For example, Jeffrey Dahmer and Ted Bundy were both serial killers. Yet, Dahmer was motivated by the need for companionship and love, however distorted and

delusional; while Bundy was motivated by nothing more than a sadistic desire to inflict pain. Thus, Bundy is further along the continuum of dark psychology than Dahmer, even though both were serial killers.

5. Dark psychology assumes that all people have the innate capacity for violence. While animals share this capacity, they employ violence to serve the needs of the predator-prey relationship in the natural order. Because human beings have evolved beyond that state, yet still retain the innate capacity for violence, this capacity is distorted in human psychology and may be used to act in violence without a practical purpose.

Following are four profiles of criminal personality types that have been identified by law enforcement officials and clinical psychologists as exhibiting behavior that exists on the far-right end of the dark continuum:

Arsonists: Arsonists are obsessed with setting fires and commonly have experienced a history of sexual and/or physical abuse. Their dark psychological personality traits are evident in their tendency to live apart from social groups. This isolation tends to further accelerate their decline into self-obsession, which enables them to more easily support their fascination with setting fires. They generally experience a sense of pleasure and happiness when they see their target structures burn.

Necrophiliacs: These are people who exhibit a sexual attraction to corpses. Because necrophiliacs have a difficult time establishing emotional or social bonds with others, their psychological and emotional development is disrupted, and as they move along the Dark Continuum, their attraction to the inanimateness of corpses intensifies.

Serial killers: The FBI defines a serial killer as anyone who commits "a series of three or more killings, not less than one of which was committed within the United States, having common characteristics such as to suggest the reasonable possibility that the crimes were committed by the same actor or actors" (Nuccitelli, 2006).

Clinical psychologists have found that serial killers are motivated by the psychological gratification that can only be achieved through brutality and killing gives them a feeling of released tension and increased power.

iPredators. This group of predators represents a new development in the field of dark psychology because ICT has been in use for only a relatively short amount of time.

Practical and Historical Overview

The foundations of the study of dark psychology are not modern. The models of classical comedy and tragedy during the height of the Greek Empire illustrate an understanding of this uniquely human capacity even during ancient times. The comedies and tragedies of ancient Greek theater were used as a means for society to experience catharsis—a collective exercise in which social bonding occurred by the creation and release of social tensions as a means of resolving societal conflicts.

But what is at the heart of this classical method of employing art as a means of regulating society is society's need to be regulated because of the unique capacity of human beings to act in ways that are destructive and harmful without any apparent practical purpose or necessity. This capacity is what clinical psychologists refer to as dark psychology.

Consider that species other than humans, such as lions, wolves, bears, or birds of prey, may track, target, hunt, and kill smaller, less powerful animals, such as deer, cattle, sheep, rabbits, and rodents. Yet, the reason for this predatory behavior is necessity, not cruelty or malevolence. In addition, when predatory animals hunt, they are likely to target the most vulnerable and the weakest, not out of any sense of meanness or malice, but because engaging with a weaker opponent involves less risk and less effort. Thus, the violence and destruction of natural predators serves practical needs—to feed themselves and their young in an effort to propagate their species.

Especially in the modern world, human beings have the advantage of education, positions of professional employment, the ability to grow and cultivate food, advanced language and communication systems, and a complex and interconnected system of world government, law, finance, and banking. As a result, there is no practical reason for any human being to engage in any act of predation or violence to secure the goals of food, shelter, and propagation. In fact, because the system of laws punishes violence, such actions are actually detrimental to achieving these goals.

These habits and systems of living are unique to the human species, so it is reasonable to assume that they may require responses and abilities among the human members of society that are also unique. For example, lions and wolves are incapable of becoming doctors, plumbers, mechanics, or politicians, nor will they ever have any interest in doing so. These occupations are unique to the human species.

It is tempting to argue that human beings have developed their unique capacity for dark psychology as a means of propagating their survival in this unique environment. Take for instance a business man who cheats on his taxes to gain an advantage in the business world, a lawyer who alters evidence to win a case, or a politician who lies to his constituents to win an election may be compared to the abilities of wild bears who hunt and kill deer or other game. Yet, animals in the wild never engage in predatory conduct that is marked by cruelty, maliciousness, or greed. Doing so would lead to their extinction.

We may understand that a business owner or banking professional would use every tool at his or her disposal to gain a competitive advantage. We may even understand the tendency among some professionals to work around laws rather than follow them when they see an economic advantage in doing so—when no real harm results, there is a practical goal that justifies the apparent abuse.

But often, criminal activity in human society does not have any practical justification. Within the unique sphere of human experience, dark psychology itself is a unique phenomenon. Defined broadly, it is the capacity for destructive and harmful behavior that serves no practical purpose whatsoever.

While all human beings have the capacity for dark psychology, many people do not act on these dark urges, choosing instead to channel that energy toward more productive and useful activities. Some people, however, do act on these dark urges to inflict gratuitous pain and harm on others.

Among those who are governed by dark psychology rather than by rational psychology, there is a continuum of deviant behavior ranging from mild forms of manipulation and dishonesty, usually motivated by some type of personal or financial gain; to acts of physical violence; and at the most extreme end of the spectrum, the movement toward the "Dark Singularity," in which a person's psychology becomes so compromised by and addicted to deviant, aberrant, criminal, and malevolent misconduct that it becomes impossible for them ever to return to a rational mental state.

Historical tales of serial killers like Jack the Ripper remind us that this human failure is not new. Unfortunately, modern society appears to have embraced, at least to some limited degree, a complete rejection of all morality and social norms. The anonymity and access to power and information made possible by the invention of the internet has given these elements resources to establish for themselves a viable, permanent presence in human society. Understanding the nature and function of dark psychology has become an indispensable tool for anyone working to achieve success.

Before considering any further what "dark psychology" means, it may be more helpful to consider what "normal" means. Many historians and literary theorists have made the case that the evolution of human civilization has been accompanied by a steady erosion of social, moral, and cultural norms.

The word "more" (with the "e" pronounced as a long a, i.e., MOR-ay) is used to describe the social rules society enforces to encourage acceptable behavior. Many college graduates may remember taking a course from a sociology professor who required as a homework assignment that they deliberately identify and violate a more, then write a paper about the consequences. At one time, it was not uncommon for visitors to a college campus to enter an elevator and find themselves joined by an apparently well-adjusted and successful college student who, for no apparent reason, faced the back of the elevator rather than the doors, thereby forcing uncomfortable and prolonged eye contact. This example of social deviance is very mild and can be viewed as even less threatening when we consider that it occurred in the context of a supervised experiment in the controlled and benign environment of a postsecondary educational institute.

Literature and humanities professors may help students examine this phenomenon in greater, and often more graphic and unforgettable, detail. For example, a pre-internet era literature course at a state university in California examined the transformation of cultural norms from 17th century France up through late 20th century America. In this course, the French novel, La Princesse de Clèves, was used to set a ground floor of social norms.

This novel portrays the life of a young woman living in the court of Henry II. Her mother had raised her with the greatest discipline to rise to the height of French society. As she enters adulthood, she is escorted to court to secure a prospect for marriage among the young noblemen. She eventually marries a young prince.

Already at this point in the novel, by today's standards, the main character of the novel would be considered successful beyond the reach of most people. However, her life does not proceed according to the ease and happiness we might expect. Instead, royal intrigue, gossip, and power struggles complicate matters. Although no actual wrongdoing ever really takes place, the young princess's hopes and ambitions are ultimately destroyed by the mere suspicion of infidelity. She is ultimately motivated by her sense of duty and obligation to enter a convent, where she dies in obscurity.

The course then uses literary works from intervening eras to trace the decline in the standards of human civilization from the virtuous heights depicted in La Princesse de Clèves through the dawn of the Industrial Revolution and ultimately to modern society at the end of 20th century America. The endpoint is illustrated by the violence, decadence, chaos, and alienation depicted in the late 20th century American novel, Looking for Mr. Goodbar.

In this novel, a young schoolteacher, who, like the princess in the novel, is an accomplished woman occupying an enviable position, is also seeking a prospect. However, her environment—the singles bars of New York City—is far removed from the royal court of 17th century France. Like the princess in the novel, she too suffers a tragic fate at a young age when she is murdered by a young man, she has met on one of her social outings.

Thus, defining social norms has become increasingly challenging, and many people have made the case that those norms are eroding as humanity progresses through its evolutionary cycles. We may refer to this tendency to develop destructive, negative, or harmful behavior as "dark psychology." All of the works depicting this trend mentioned above existed prior to the invention of digital technology and the internet.

The emergence of iPredators as a class of offenders identified by clinical psychologists underscores the importance of understanding this area of psychology. New technology has expanded the power and speed through which dark psychology has found a way to manifest itself among many segments of human society; ICT has also magnified the degree to which such lifestyles have made themselves potentially viable, long-term means of living.

The following chart illustrates the differences in the psychological makeup between well-adjusted people with healthy psychology and those who exhibit predominantly dark psychological traits:

So, dark psychology, in its most general sense, is that part of human psychology that drives people to act in ways that are harmful or deviant. As we have seen, this deviant behavior may range from deliberate but harmless violations of social norms in an educational environment, to mean-spirited rumors spread to defeat opponents, to violent predatory crimes that end lives and lead to severe and long-lasting trauma.

Chapter 2. The Dark Triad

Dark triad is a key concept that ties together all aspects of dark psychology. The dark triad in a nutshell is the theme that houses the three most destructive and harmful psychological personality traits known to man in the concurrent pages, well shall seek to bring these traits to light and Better understand them for adequate preparation against them by the time we are done, you will realize that all other themes of dark psychology stem from this very theme. These traits are psychopathy, narcissism and Machiavellianism. The majority of individuals by the mention of these very traits will have a stereotypic description of psychopath as a murderous person, and a narcissist as a human who is just obsessed with themselves. There is however much more to these antisocial disorders than just the stereotypes. Each of these concepts must be respected and understood for their power to become apparent.

Machiavellianism

This is a technique that traces its origins from the famous political philosopher known as Machiavelli. His established works on influence and political power, "the prince", Machiavelli shares with the rest of the world his version of ideas, principles, and tactics that have saved the purpose of a sort of blueprint for those individuals who might be looking for influence throughout the course of history. Based on this, we then ask ourselves what this Machiavellian person actually is and how he comes about. What puts this particular tactic on the map is basically the manipulator's affinity to only focus on one's self-interest at all times, the exercise of ruthless power and cruelty, one's understanding of the importance of image and the perception and superficial appearance in a nutshell, Machiavellian individuals are people whose approach to life is widely strategic. Meaning that, the ramifications and consequences that they take are usually well thought out and assessed in terms of how they might end up impacting their lives if they do it in a particular way .you may simply identify a Machiavellian individual since their speech often revolves around something like, "how will this benefit me, and how will my public reputation be impacted by this result?"

Machiavellian individuals are pros at doing that which personally serves their interests while at the same time skilfully managing to maintain the best public image without anyone being the wiser. Perhaps one of the biggest examples of one such individual is that of the former president of the United States, bill Clinton. He succumbed to his sexual desires while in office time and time again, while at the same time managed to keep the people's admiration for him stronger than ever. This is really an advantage he had over majority of politicians with the same lifestyle but is frowned upon by the public. Another example in the political arena is also that of President Barrack Obama, and George W Bush. Barrack Obama while in office cultivated and capitalized on his love for peace while Bush solidified his image as that of a guy who always had war on his mind. Obama was able to manipulate the masses building a public perception that served his one interest evil bush did to even try. This is despite the very fact that both of these presidents were as militant as the following president. This is a very powerful lesson of what people perceive VS what the actual reality of things is.

Psychopathy

To be able to tell you in black and white what psychopathy really is would be difficult but the vary basic definition of what psychopathy really is ,or rather who a psychopath really is, is that particular individual who seems to be suffering from a type of psychological disorder which heavily involve a superficial charm, impulsivity and a lack of commonly held "human" emotions such as empathy and remorse .these psychopaths can be regarded as the most dangerous people on the face of the earth as they are the best examples of two faced sons of bitches. Pardon my language. When majority of people hear the mention of these individuals, the first image that usually comes to mind is of a haggard looking individual wielding a machete and wearing a mask like John Wayne Agency. But the reality of their identity is far from this. They are most likely to be very handsome strangers who win over their victims by being just the right amount of charming, before eventually ruining or even ending their victim's lives. Surprisingly, based on a series of tests, experiments, and observations, it has been discovered that there exists a high number of these individuals at the very helm of the business world. A majority of people are just now beginning to view psychopathy as more of a problem to the whole society that for the very psychopaths owns selves. They are usually programmed in such a way that they can survive in any field they chose to go into. This is mainly attributed to their indifferent views they have regarding normal human feeling of love, compassion and so forth.

Narcissism

If you ask anyone who they think a narcissus is, I can bet on it that the most likely answer you are likely to receive is that of an individual who simply loves themselves. This is along the correct lines but not accurate enough, particularly when narcissism is understood through the dark triad lens. Without being a narcissist, you can have self-love. So, what are some of the differences between a highly self-esteemed individual and someone who is narcissistic to the extent that they are regarded in the Dark Triad range? Someone who meets narcissism's medical diagnostic requirements, to the point that they are deemed to have a psychological disorder, is likely to continuously display a variety of the following characteristics. They are usually captives of the inflated sense of self-worth which manifests itself f in a number of ways .these include seeing their lives as the most special and important to have ever existed., seeing that they're of a biter spaces hire in status than that of "normal people". This behavior often reflects their sense of self-worth.

Narcissists are likely to have an excessively inflated self-worth, such as seeing their life as special and one of the most important in history, often the most important. Narcissists are not, in their own minds, only special—they are superior. They are a better species of person, higher in status than "normal" people. Their behavior reflects their sense of self-worth. Some of narcissism's prevalent outward manifestations are an inability in any manner to tolerate criticism or dissent. The need to be flattered is similar to this need to be agreed. Narcissists need continuous praise, endorsement, and appreciation and tend to organize their life in a manner that provides them continuous access to others who meet this need.

Having looked at the base of this particular behemoth theme of dark psychology, let us now dive in headfirst into how the dark triad manifests itself into the behaviors of these indifferent human beings.

Machiavellian characteristics

What was explained above, we know that a Machiavellian person is a political schemer who is mainly concerned border lining obsessed with his public image. These particular groups of individuals are considered to be the most cold-hearted in their pursuit of self-interest above all else. What then could be said about the behavior of these types of individuals? Due to their master level skill of masking their true intentions from the public eye, their behaviors might be abetted hard to decipher.

For most individuals who do not fulfil Machiavellianism's clinical definition, their public persona is generally a reflection of their true personal self. Everyone polishes their picture and conduct in public a little, but in general, the outward picture of most people is nothing more than a polished portrait of who they really are. They often have a fine line as to what they truly are and the person who they often pottery themselves to be in the public eye. Perhaps the best example to be given here is that of serial killers. The best has often been able to escape the grip of the law because of their outward image being the furthest thing from their morbid fascinations. The most famous example that can be given on this is that of renowned serial killer, Ted Bundy. He was a very handsome man according to those who knew him. He was also very eloquent and just wall presented that no one imagines him to have a single bad bone in his body. This is what enabled him to murder an upwards of 30 women before he was eventually caught.

Examples of such a distinction between intent and appearance can be found in areas less extreme than serial murder. There are countless tales of leaders in the world of business who manage to ruthlessly cut jobs and pursue profit over people whenever possible. In terms of Machiavellianism, the very best of these bosses can actually get individuals to purchase into the idea that they behave by necessity or even compassion! Such rulers are almost role models for those who only want to serve their own wishes while simultaneously appearing to be a "person of the individuals."

A willingness to exploit people is another hallmark of Machiavellian individuals. Let us look at an example to have a better understanding of this. A newcomer in a particular office who possesses these Machiavellian traits would see each individual colleague, boss or team member as a resource or piece of a puzzle to use and utilize. The Machiavellian person would see a sequence of strategic threats and weaknesses to handle, exploit, or neutralize instead of seeing others as fellow human beings. This is a big component of the reason why Machiavellians are so conscious of how they find themselves. They understand that this outward depiction is the key to exercising impact and exploiting everybody they come across effectively.

Another characteristic of Machiavellian people is the instillation of fear in the people around them. This comes straight from "The Prince" which urges individuals to simultaneously be both feared and loved. At the same moment, this notion of the desirability of being loved and feared is directly related to the Machiavellian characteristic of dividing a public and private perception. In the very individuals who would truly pretend to feel greater love than fear as a consequence, the ideal Machiavellian can inspire fear and obedience.

Psychopathic characteristics

It is in all aspects to know how this group of individuals manifest themselves so as to detect them early and putting up the necessary defenses against them. Charm is one of a psychopathic person's most prevalent behaviors. It must be understood that this charm is superficial rather than profound, real charm. If you think of a truly charming individual from your lifetime, you will probably acknowledge that they have favorable characteristics that underpin outward behavioral displays. However, if an n individual genuinely displays a charming persona as an expression of kindness, they should not be labelled as psychopaths. Psychopaths can show all the outward indications of charm such as physical appeal, obvious warmth, and interest in others. The inward motive behind these outward displays is why it's such a red flag. Psychopaths see charm as part of an equation. The manipulator usually asks himself as to whether if displaying a particular emotion towards the victim makes them feel in a particular euphoric way and also if the result will prove to be advantageous or themselves. They are very calculative people who are numb to normal human feelings. Lying is another trait that really makes psychopaths really stands out. We all lie in our day to day lives. This doesn't necessarily mean that we are all psychopaths. However, it can show a psychopathic personality when coupled with other characteristics. Lying comes for a psychopath as naturally as breathing for most individuals who are psychologically healthy. A psychopath can convincingly present the reality in a specific time as anything they need it to be. Also, psychopaths do not demonstrate outward indications of lying because they do not have any emotional attachment or emotions of shame, guilt or excitement about their lies. Lying is just "doing what's required at the moment" for psychopaths.

Another signature aspect of psychopathy is a lack of impulse control. Most individuals have processes and inner controls that stop them from acting rashly. These mechanisms of prevention are lacking for a psychopath. If a psychopath sees a chance they want to exploit, they will behave without hesitation or a second thought. This may require murdering someone they want to kill, violating someone they want to rape, or stealing something they want to steal. This cruel impulsiveness is what makes psychopaths in areas such as the army and company globe some of the most efficient individuals. Automatic adoption of decisive intervention is a feature that much non-psychopaths lack, and this absence are, in fact, detrimental to life advancement.

Another characteristic that distinguishes psychopaths from no psychopathic people is a lack of remorse. Many individuals who have committed atrocious acts, such as murder, feel a profound feeling of guilt and shame about what they have accomplished because of these emotions and even take their own lives. Psychopaths do not choose to be remorseful— they are physically unable to do so. Asking a psychopath to feel remorse is like asking to listen to music from a deaf individual. A lack of guilt is closely associated with a lack of remorse. Usually humans feel guilty when they break some kind of moral standard they value personally. Since psychopaths do not believe correctly or wrongly, only helpful or unnecessary, guilt is an alien notion for them. The nearest thing that a psychopath may convey to guilt or remorse is regret that they have not performed their psychopathic acts to their own high standards.

Narcissistic characteristics

One of the most prevalent characteristics in all almost all narcissists is the fantasies of their absolute power and elevated sense of importance. Most of these individuals lay blame to the constant praise they got as children while talking about these fantasies as adults these individuals will still demand praise from all around hem since they have nurtured the feeling of being most important of their peers to the maximum.

The inflated sense of self-worth experienced internally by narcissists also has consequences for their external reality. This typically manifests in two ways— the need for consent and praise, and criticism or rejection hate. For the narcissistic ego, praise and consensus are like oxygen, while criticism and dissent are like poison. Picture a dictator in a hermit state in order to comprehend what narcissism looks like when taken to its logical conclusion. Such individuals request worship from those over whom they have authority, statue building in their likeness, and full obedience and recognition. Any act of dissent or disagreement shall be punished quickly and brutally. North Korea would be an ideal contemporary illustration of narcissism's extreme manifestation. That nation's rulers request reverence like gods and execute and torture anyone who even dares to convey a thought or concept that is not entirely consistent with formal doctrine of the state.

Chapter 3.Dark Persuasion

Persuasion happens everywhere in day-to-day life. It can be seen in how we interact with others, leaning in to persuade people to keep talking while ignoring them in hopes that they will be persuaded to go away. We persuade others to help by asking them and pleading our case, or we persuade people to do something through suggesting it. What makes persuasion dark versus regular persuasion, and how does dark persuasion work? If you want to understand why dark persuasion is so manipulative, you must first understand what it entails, as well as how it differs from harmless persuasion.

Defining Dark Persuasion

At its simplest, persuasion is the act of coaxing or influencing someone into doing or believing something that they did not do or believe prior. Think of asking someone to do something that would never have occurred to them before. Perhaps you ask your partner to help you carry something because it is too heavy, and your partner has not yet offered help. If your partner then decides to carry something for you, you have successfully persuaded them. There is nothing inherently manipulative or wrong about doing this—you are simply asking for help and your partner obliges.

Dark persuasion, then, adds a level of darkness. Remember, darkness implies selfishness or harm. The propensity for darkness is the propensity to doing things for one's own selfish interest with no regard of what it may or may not do to those around the manipulator. They do not care if people get hurt, betrayed, or upset. The only thing that matters to people who have a propensity for darkness or dark psychology is that one's own wants and needs are met.

Taking those two definitions, of darkness and of persuasion, you can then infer that dark persuasion is the art of influencing people to act in a way that is primarily or only beneficial to the manipulator with no regard for those being manipulated. Anything that the manipulator attempts to get from others is selfishly motivated. This selfishness, this darkness, is what makes dark persuasion so dangerous or harmful to others.

Persuasion vs. Dark Persuasion

If persuasion is acceptable, but dark persuasion is harmful, what is the real difference, you may ask. The difference lies in the intention. Persuasion, by and large, does not seek to inflict harm, and if anything, often seeks to better both the person doing the persuading and the person being persuaded. Oftentimes when trying to persuade someone, you are doing so because you believe it would be better, and this is from a good spot, seeking to benefit the other person as well. You are not trying to convince the other person to do something for your own benefit, and only your own benefit.

Ultimately, the one-sided selfishness is what differentiates the two from each other. Persuasion is not necessary but can be, selfish, but dark persuasion always is. Dark persuasion is almost always one-sided, though the other person may believe there is some sort of benefit to him or her as well. In contrast, persuasion often seeks to balance benefits of all involved, attempting to spread as much good as possible. All parties involved in normal persuasion usually benefit in some way, shape, or form, but only the manipulator benefits in dark persuasion. Dark persuasion does not concern itself with morality, whereas persuasion does. The dark persuader does not care about right or wrong, but the persuader does.

How Dark Persuasion Works

Persuasion, and therefore dark persuasion, works through seven elements. These elements enable you to influence other people, no matter whether you seek to genuinely persuade someone with the best of intentions or you wish to darkly persuade someone into the behavior you know they would not necessarily care for. Understanding these seven elements is crucial to understanding exactly how to persuade others.

Reciprocity

Reciprocity is the idea that when someone helps or gives you something, you should return the favor. Even if it is as simple as someone smiling at you, you should smile back. No matter how big or small, the favor should be returned. This typically works in everyone's favor when everyone reciprocates, because everyone sees benefits. If Alice asks Brenda for help moving furniture in exchange for homemade cookies and Brenda agrees to do so, the future time that Brenda needs help with something, Alice is going to be more likely to volunteer or agree to help. We inherently want to help others who help us; it is part of our wiring as a social species.

However, this idea of reciprocity also applies in dark persuasion. If you seek to tap into dark persuasion, you are going to seek to create a sense of obligation in your target. You will do something for the other person with the intent of cashing in on the favor you feel you are owed. Many people are likely to give in to this notion, as well, and will oftentimes, even if begrudgingly, attempt to reciprocate.

The idea with dark manipulation is to offer a small favor, typically something that does not take much of your time or energy, and then shortly after, request a favor in return. The shorter the time between you doing a favor and asking for a favor, the more likely it is that the answer will be yes, even with favors that are exponentially larger. For example, if you offer to cover your friend's coffee, insisting it is no big deal when you know that he is struggling with money while you are out, you can turn around and ask your friend to help you by babysitting all evening while you go out on a date with your spouse. The reciprocity is not even between the two—all you did was buy a cheap coffee, but you are asking your friend to give up several hours in return. Say your date is set to last four hours, and you spent $3.50 on the coffee: This is essentially paying your friend the equivalent of $0.88/hour if you were to calculate out work for pay. This may sound like a fantastic price to pay for childcare for you, but your friend ends up caring for your children for well below minimum wage, and is honestly, probably at a loss after factoring in food that the children will inevitably ask for during a four-hour window. At this point, your friend, who is already struggling to make ends meet, actually lost some money in return for drinking a cheap mocha from a café.

Consistency and Commitment

Consistency is important within persuasion because of three key factors: It is valued, creates a schedule that can be used to manage all of one's many responsibilities, and it can simplify situations that are otherwise difficult to juggle due to having a routine. This means that consistency, in effect, makes people's daily tasks more streamlined. People are able to get through everything easier when they have a set routine that enables them to meet all of their responsibilities that has proven effective in the past.

The consistency in routine allows for reliability as well. Someone who is consistent is typically also quite reliable because of his or her routine. Therefore, someone who is consistent becomes easy to persuade. One that person has agreed to do something for you, you can be certain they will follow through due to their own skills at self-motivating to remain consistent. In dark persuasion, you can take this to mean that once someone who is consistent has said they will do something, they will motivate themselves to do so, even if, halfway through, they realize that it is something that they have no desire to do, or is something that does not quite line up with their own belief systems.

Going hand-in-hand with consistency comes commitment. Those who are consistent typically follow through with commitments no matter what. They self-motivate to get the job done due to their consistency. Those who have proven themselves consistent typically will continue to follow that pattern, believing remaining consistent and reliable is integral to which they are as a person. This self-motivation is, in essence, a form of self-persuasion. By simply getting a commitment, you may not even have to do the persuasion part; the other person will do the work for you.

This means that once you bind this person to do something, it will almost absolutely happen. Commitments are valued and not taken lightly. Even if you do find that the other person is balking at the agreement and seeming as though he or she may back out of the arrangement, appealing to that commitment, reminding the other person that they had promised or otherwise committed him- or herself to completing the commitment is often enough to keep them in line.

Within dark persuasion, then, by earning a commission, particularly from someone consistent, you are able to then ensure that you do not have to work hard to hold the other person accountable. Ultimately, those interested in dark persuasion and covert manipulation seek to get results with the least amount of effort, so by getting someone that you know is consistent and dedicated to meeting commitments, you are able to lessen your workload. You know that you are not likely to need to nag at the other person to follow through, which means you do not have to do as much follow up work.

Social Proof

Social proof is, in essence, herd mentality. It is the idea that people feel the constraints of social pressure demanding that they act in a certain way. It is the feeling of being obligated to do something simply because society dictates that is the way things are done, particularly in situations in which someone is unfamiliar. When unsure about the situation, people tend to follow the lead of those around them, feeling the pressure to conform. They assume that those around them, who seem to be moving around seamlessly, know what is supposed to be done, and therefore decide to mimic them in hopes of behaving appropriately.

This phenomenon is even more pronounced when the individual who is unsure about the situation is able to closely relate to those who are acting, to whom the individual decides to conform. This can be seen in various experiments. In one such experiment, researchers joined a charity campaign that went door to door to get donations. When the list of donators had more names on it, the people being asked to donate were typically more likely to donate, particularly when the person being solicited recognized names on the donor list as being known neighbors, friends, or peers.

This relates to persuasion because it involves what is seen as horizontal rather than vertical; at its core, this means that people are more likely to be influenced by their peers than their superiors. They are more likely to adopt the behaviors of people they identify with than those who have power.

Within dark persuasion, then, this concept could be used to influence people to conform. If the predator were to fabricate a list of donators, for example, he would be able to better convince people to donate. Likewise, the predator could fabricate situations in which the target is alongside people who are acting the way the predator desires, allowing for the predator to influence the target's actions without it ever becoming obvious.

Likable

Imagine that two people, one who you like, and the others who you do not, ask you to do the same thing. Who do you help, if anyone? The most likely answer is that you will help the person you like. People tend to agree to help people they like and are far more likely to say yes if they like the person attempting to persuade them. The question, then, is who do people like? How do people decide who the like and dislike?

Ultimately, the answer involves three factors that determine how likable someone is to us:

- People with whom we can identify closely

- People who complement or flatter us

- People who are willing to cooperate in order to attain similar, mutual goals or outcomes

Understanding what people like and naturally gravitate toward gives manipulators an idea of how to act in order to get inside a desired target's inner circle. The manipulator learns that, in order to get a yes, he or she should aim to be relatable, compliment the target, and identify common goals, even if those common goals are falsified by the manipulator to create some sort of semblance of a connection.

Once those three standards have been met, the dark persuader is far more likely to get desired results when asking someone to do something. The persuader has tapped into unconscious biases and tendencies in order to get desired results.

Authority

By and large, people defer to authority and are more likely to do whatever someone asks if they see clear signs of authority presented to them. For example, a person may listen to what a nurse has to say about care at home but may not follow through. If that same person were told the same thing by a doctor whose lab coat declared them the head of the ER department, however, they would be far more likely to do as told. This is because the person unconsciously defers to higher authorities. In the person's mind, the nurse may not be as worthy of being an authority as the doctor who is the head of the emergency room, even though the information provided is exactly the same.

In terms of being able to persuade others, then, this implies that it is important to cue that the predator is an authority in some way. You can convince people to buy products if you have a business degree hanging on the wall, and you can sway someone by using your credentials with your name on nameplates, business cards, and other identifying items. Consider if someone talked to you about what you should do with your insurance on your car—would you be more inclined to listen to a random person in casual clothes, or someone wearing a shirt emblazoned with the logo of a popular, well-known insurance company? The answer is the one who has identified themselves as a representative of an insurance company. You would assume they are an authority on the product if their shirt marks them as someone involved with the insurance business.

The dark persuaders, then, could take this a step further. Either through misrepresenting experience, or even lying about credentials, they are able to be seen as more reliable. They may discuss some reason they have more working knowledge over a situation, and because of that, they should be seen as a default authority on the matter.

Scarcity

People always want what they cannot have. Because oftentimes, people see the proverbial grass is greener on the other side, by imposing scarcity on a product, demand goes up. If an unpopular item is being removed from a menu, people will suddenly want it more, until it is gone, at which point, that item that never sold well in the first place is suddenly missed. Many restaurants follow similar structures, offering items for a limited time only, although realistically, they would be able to produce enough to meet demand if they chose to. Hype for the item is built through the exclusive nature of it—because it is limited, more people want to try it before they lose the opportunity forever.

When it comes to persuading others, then, keeping scarcity in mind can be particularly useful. Not only should a predator make sure to tout benefits toward what people can gain by going along with the predator's plan, but also what may be lost if the plan is not followed. Emphasizing the temporary nature of the deal, as well as what the loss of the deal will entail. People will be far more likely to go along with the plan if they feel like they stand to lose something if they do not do it.

Chapter 4.Dark Seduction Techniques

The first approach that we will look at is known as the indirect approach. One mistake that you may see in conventional dating is that one or both parties will offer an icebreaker, one that is usually unappealing and cheesy, when they try to introduce themselves to someone new. They may say something like "You look pretty," "Nice eyes," or "Good song, right?"

Why are these icebreakers so bad? It is likely that the victim of your seduction has heard these countless times, and as soon as they hear them, they will be turned off and not want to talk to you at all. When the seducer uses such a bad line, it often leaves the impression that they are unappealing and bland, and no one wants to waste their time on a relationship with that kind of person.

With the indirect opener, the seducer is throwing in a breath of fresh air compared to the opening lines we talked about before. An indirect opener is going to be an icebreaker that will start the social interaction but won't convey any sexual intent. Often it is going to be posed as an "intriguing question."

A good example of this would be when the seducer asks something like "Settle this for me or my buddies over there – do men or women lie more?" This is a different way to open up and talk with the other person and can start up a new conversation. And it shows the victim that the seducer is very interesting and is interested in a good conversation.

These indirect openers have the advantage of eliminating the possibility of rejection. The person who uses this kind of opener is not really offering themselves to the victim of the seduction. It is basically impossible to reject something that wasn't even offered, so it takes that part out of the equation.

Another technique to use with dark seduction is social proof. People who are popular are going to be more attractive compared to those who aren't. It is a human instinct to assume that if another person is liked by a lot of people, then there must be something that makes that person likable.

Social proof is an example of showing is more powerful than telling. Many people will try to talk about their success or their popularity, but this isn't a good idea.

It is going to seem like you are bragging and can be a big turnoff to the other person. It is better to simply make sure that you are at a table or near others who are interesting. This is going to convey your social value, without seeming like you are showing off in the process.

Of course, social proof can be used for devious purposes. Think about a psychological seducer who is at a club or a bar. They see a girl that they want to seduce. Rather than directly approaching this person, they will decide to approach someone else and start a conversation with them, before moving over to their original target. This can remove the idea that the seducer is lonely, and it can sometimes spark a little jealousy that works in advantage to the seducer.

You can also work with a frame of leading to help with dark seduction. Many times, you will find that the people you meet are happy to be led. Indecisiveness is one of the least attractive qualities in others. If you are able to show that you are decisive, you can automatically get the attention of others.

There are several ways that the dark seducer can show their decisiveness and that they have the ability to lead. Some of these could be physically moving around a venue, making the suggestion that it is time to change venues and not being scared to disagree with what someone else has said. Many men try to be indecisive around their victim because they don't' want to come off as weak. This is going to work against them. A dark seducer knows that they need to be decisive if they want to have any chance with the other person.

In addition to some of the techniques that we have talked about above, there are some seducers who are able to harness some of the other dark psychology traits, such as the use of psychopathy, in order to reach their romantic goals. For example, one trademark of psychopathy is the ability of the seducer not to feel any fear when they interact with other people.

Many times, a man or a woman is going to be paralyzed by fear, especially when there is a chance for rejection by someone, they are interested in. A dark seducer is not going to have this fear because they just don't understand the fear at all. Even if you are not a dark manipulator and you don't regularly use dark seduction, you can use this idea.

A psychological seducer is going to learn, over time, that it is better to be the one who tried and failed rather than the one who didn't have any confidence to try in the first place.

Why Are Dark Seducers So Dangerous?

A dark seducer can be a formidable foe. They know exactly how to get the other person, their victim, to fall in love with them. But the problem comes with the fact that the dark seducer really isn't in love with the other person. There is something that the dark seducer wants out of the relationship. This could be companionship because they don't like to be alone, sex, or something else. But they are usually not looking for love at all.

As soon as the victim of this seduction doesn't provide the thing that their seducer wants, the seducer is going to leave. So, if the victim starts to feel that they are being used and withholds sex from the seducer, the seducer will simply leave the relationship and move on to their future victim.

The seducer has no worries about the other partner in the relationship. A true seducer is only going to see the other person as a tool, something that helps the seducer get the pleasure that they want.

As soon as that tool stops doing the job that it's supposed to, the seducer will move on to find a new person to do the work for them.

A dark seducer may move quickly between one relationship to the other, or they may even stay in a relationship for a long time. It all depends on the situation and how long the seducer is able to keep the victim under their control. Some victims stand up for themselves pretty quickly. The longer the victim is under the control of the dark seducer, the harder it is for them to leave.

This doesn't mean that the dark seducer has learned how to love their victim. It simply means that the dark seducer has become used to the way that things are, and they will use their powers and their mind control techniques in order to keep the victim right where they are.

How to Avoid Dark Seduction

It is important for you to be aware of dark seduction. While some men may choose to use some of the ideas of dark seduction in order to help them gain some confidence, avoid some issues with their fear of rejection, and make it easier for them to meet women, there are many that will use these techniques because they don't really care about the other person at all.

They have specific goals that they want to reach in the relationship, and they will get there, no matter who gets hurt in the process.

If you do end up getting into one of these relationships, it can be devastating. The dark manipulator is really skilled at using the dark seduction techniques to get what they want. They will find a victim who is vulnerable, and they will present the right solution that the victim needs at that time. For example, they may find a victim who just got out of a major relationship, and they will step in to feel the need of that victim to not be lonely any longer.

The seducer is going to be charming, fun, and the perfect person for that victim. The victim may feel like they have found their soulmate, but the seducer is just there to get what they want out of the relationship. Sure, it may last for some time, but as soon as the victim is no longer meeting the needs of the seducer, the seducer will be gone.

This will leave the victim hurt and broken. They may have overly trusted the seducer (because the seducer is skilled at reading the victim and knew exactly what to do and say to gain that trust and get what they want), and now they are broken. They may go through depression and anxiety and even have trouble trusting others in the future.

Because of all these negatives that come with dark seduction, it is important to watch out for the signs. If you run into dark seduction with a narcissist or with a psychopath, it is even more important to watch for the signs. These individuals are not there to care about what the other person wants.

They simply look out for themselves; they feel that they deserve what they want, and they don't have the capacity to care about how it is going to harm the other person.

Due to the way that the relationship was started, including the romance, attraction, the mutual feeling that you found a soulmate (all created by the seducer to get what they want), when things start to take a lot of wrong turns, it is likely to be too late for you, the victim, to walk away. This can be especially true if you went into that particular picture without a good idea of what you wanted in the relationship. Without this clear picture, you would not have the determination to walk away from that relationship when it didn't meet your expectations.

This is why you must always make sure that you know what you want to get out of the relationship before one begins. This will help you be prepared if the relationship becomes something else because you will be able to see when it is going away from your chosen course. You will give yourself a chance to see it for what it is before you damage your self-worth so much where you will stay in that relationship and accept the bad treatment.

This can be hard. Many times, we feel that we need a relationship like we are not worth anything unless we are in a relationship with someone else. Then, when we are not in a relationship, we are going to feel like something is missing, and we jump into the first relationship that comes available. This is where the issues will start.

Before you jump into the upcoming relationship, it is important to take some time to soul search.

Remember that there is nothing wrong with not being in a relationship all the time. Taking some time for yourself and really exploring where you are at that time in your life and what you would like to happen in your future relationship can make a difference.

This gives you a good idea of what kind of relationship you want to be in. You won't just jump into the future relationship because you are needy or because you worry about being alone. You will have specific goals in mind, and if you feel the relationship isn't going in the right direction, you will be able to step out before the dark seducer gets too deep and tries to take control over you.

The first thing that you should do here is to start with some deep thinking and even some soul-searching and decide on the details of the relationship that you are looking to enjoy at that time in your life. Describe what you want out of the other person in this partnership. Describe how you want to feel in this relationship. Set out some clear boundaries and then make sure that you understand why you have these boundaries.

Chapter 5.Hypnosis and Its Application

We will begin by getting a clear definition of hypnosis. Experts have defined hypnosis as a considered state of mindfulness that entails focused attention together with a decreased peripheral awareness, which is denoted by an increased capacity of a participant to get back to suggestions offered to him. This construes that an individual taking part in this process enters a changed state of mind and is more vulnerable to giving in to the suggestions/options offered to him by the hypnotist. Two theory groups are widely recognized in helping to describe what happens during the period of hypnosis. The first of these two is referred to as the altered state theory. Individuals following this theory see hypnosis like a state of mind or trance, which is altered where the subject sees his awareness is rather different from what he would recognize in his normal conscious state. The second theory is the non-state theory. Individuals following this theory believe that participants undergoing hypnosis do not enter a different state of consciousness. Instead, the participants and the hypnotist work together to enter some form of imaginative role expression/enactment.

During the hypnosis process, the subject has more concentration and focus, which comes along with the new potential to powerfully focus on a specific thought or memory. While in this process, subjects can clog other external sources that they consider as a distraction to them. The hypnotized participants are likely to show an increased capability of responding to suggestions given to them, particularly when the hypnotist gives the suggestions. The process used to place the subjects into hypnosis is referred to as hypnotic induction, and it involves a sequence of instructions and suggestions used as a form of a warmup. There are various thoughts that experts have brought up over the years to try to define hypnosis. The wide range of these descriptions emanates from the fact that there exist various situations that accompany hypnosis, and there is not a single person who has similar experiences when undergoing it.

Very different statements and views have been made regarding hypnosis. Some individuals see hypnosis as very real, and they are fearful that the government, as well as people around them, may try controlling their minds. As well, there are those who do not believe that there is such a thing as hypnosis that exists at all, and they believe that it is just a sleight of hand. Probably, the thought of hypnosis as a form of mind control lies somewhere in the middle. The psychological community recognizes three stages of hypnosis. The three stages comprise of induction, susceptibility, and suggestion. Each of these stages is crucial to the hypnosis process and are deliberated on further below.

Induction

This is the first stage of hypnosis. Before the subject goes through the entire hypnosis, he is subjected to the hypnotic induction approach. Over many years, the method was believed to be employed in putting the participant into his hypnotic trance, though the definition has transformed some in the present times. Some non-state theorists see this stage to some extent differently. Rather they view this stage as a technique used to increase the subjects' expectations on what is to take place, describing their expected role, getting their concentration and focus towards the right direction, as well as any other steps needed in leading the subject into the proper course for hypnosis.

Several induction tactics are used in the hypnosis process. The most influential and well-known methods are James Braids' "eye-fixation" tactic, also referred to as "Braidism." Few variations of the Braidism approaches exist such as the Stanford Hypnotic Susceptibility Scale (SHSS). It is the most employed research tool in the hypnosis field. In order to make use of the Braid induction methods, one needs to follow several outlined steps.

Suggestion

In the hypnosis process, suggestion is the following stage. When James Braid first described hypnosis, suggestion as a term was not used. Instead, he cited this stage as an act of having the participant's conscious mind focusing on one dominant and central idea. Braid did this in a way that was to reduce or stimulate the physical functioning of the various regions on the subject's body. Then, Braid started to emphasize more and more on the use of divergent verbal and non-verbal forms of suggestion to get the subject into a hypnotic mental state.

These included using "waking suggestions" besides self-hypnosis. Hippolyte Bernheim, another renowned hypnotist, continued shifting the significance of the physical state in the hypnosis process to the psychological process, which entailed verbal suggestions. According to him, hypnotism is an induction of a supernatural condition that is irregular, and which increases the vulnerability of the idea/suggestion to the subject.

He frequently stated that the hypnotic state induced helps in facilitating the suggestion, although this may not be essential to start the vulnerability in the first place.

Modern hypnotism makes use of many different forms of suggestion to be successful. These forms may include insinuations, direct verbal suggestions, metaphors, indirect/non-verbal suggestions, and other figures of speech as well as nonverbal suggestions. Nonverbal suggestions, some of them, may be employed during the suggestion stage may include mental imagery, physical manipulation, and voice tonality. Among the distinctions that can be made in the forms of suggestion offered to the subject comprises the suggestions which are delivered with consent as well as those that are more draconian in manner.

Among the things that need to be factored regarding hypnosis is the contrast between the conscious and the unconscious mind. Several hypnotists see the stage of suggestion as a means of communication majorly directed to the subject's conscious mind. Other people in this field see it in a conflicting direction; they perceive the communication to be taking place between the unconscious or subconscious and the agent. The advocates of the initial class of thought comprised of Braid, Bernheim, as well as other architects of the Victorian age. They alleged that the ideas/suggestions were being communicated straight to the subject's conscious mind, instead of the unconscious part. In fact, Braid went further and defined the act of hypnotism as intensive attention focused on the dominant idea or suggestion. According to the individuals who follow this school of thought, most people's fear that the hypnotists can slip into their unconscious mind and try making them think and do things that are outside their control is merely impossible. The mind's nature has as well been the determining factor of the various conceptions on suggestion. Individuals who thought that the given responses are via the unconscious mind bring about the instances of using indirect ideas/suggestions. Most of these indirect suggestions, e.g., metaphors or stories, hide their envisioned meaning to hide it from the subject's conscious mind. Subliminal suggestion, a type of hypnosis, totally relies on the unconscious mind theory. This form of suggestion would not be possible if the unconscious mind was not used in hypnosis.

The contrasts between these 2 groups are quite easy to identify; those who think that the suggestions/dominant idea primarily goes to the conscious mind using direct verbal suggestions and instructions, while those who are of the thought that the instructions/suggestions primarily goes to the unconscious mind using metaphors and stories that have hidden meanings. In whichever of these two theories of thought, the subject needs to concentrate on one idea or object. This lets the subject to go into the direction required for him to get into the hypnotic condition. Once this stage has been successfully completed, the subject is able to go into the third stage known as susceptibility.

Susceptibility

Continually over the years, it has been noted that individuals react in different ways to hypnosis. There are those people who will find be able to get into a hypnotic trance easily, and they do not need to put so much effort at all into this process. Other people will get into the hypnotic trance but will only do so after a long period and with some effort used. Others may find that they cannot get into the hypnotic trance even after constant efforts they will not reach their objectives. Researchers have found out one thing that is interesting about the vulnerability/susceptibility of various subjects; is that this aspect remains constant. If maybe one has ever gotten into a hypnotic state of mind easily, then he/she is likely to remain in the same state for the rest of his/her life. Contrarily, if one has always had trouble in getting into the hypnotic state and he has never become hypnotized, then he is likely that he will never be.

Over time, there have been different models that have been developed to ascertain the participants' susceptibility to hypnosis. Several older depth scales functioned to deduce a participant's level of trance through the visible signs, which were available. These included things like the impromptu amnesia. Several modern scales are used in measuring the level of observed responsiveness or self-evaluated to the precise suggestion tests given, for instance, the direct suggestions of arm rigidness.

Deirdre Barrett conducted research that established two types of participants considered highly vulnerable to the impacts of hypnotism. The two groups include fantasizers and dissociates. The fantasizers score high ratings on the absorption scales, as they are able to suppress the inducements of the world without using hypnosis easily, spend much time daydreaming (fantasizing), had imaginative friends during their childhood, and grew up in an atmosphere where imaginative play was highly encouraged. Contrarily, are the dissociates who mostly originate from a background which is characterized by childhood abuse and trauma. The dissociates often find ways to overlook the hostile events that took place in their past and might evade into numbness. For an individual who daydreams within this group, it is likely to be in terms of becoming blank rather than having fantasies. Both groups score highly on the hypnotic susceptibility tests. There are two groups, which have the greatest rates of hypnotizability; they include those ailing dissociative identity disorder and posttraumatic stress disorder.

Applications

Hypnosis has been around for quite a long time as an idea as well as a field. Due to this fact, several applications are emerging that help in putting the hypnosis process into good use. In fact, the applications of employing hypnosis cuts across many fields like entertainment, military uses, medical uses, and self-improvement. The other fields that have started using hypnotism include education, forensics, physical therapy, rehabilitation, and sports. Artists, too, are now using hypnotism to reach particular creative purposes. An example is a surreal artist by the name Andre Breton, who has used hypnosis among several other tactics for his own creative aim. Among the fast-growing usages of hypnosis is in the area of self-improvement; numerous persons have preferred to do some self-hypnosis so as to assist them in losing weight, quit smoking as well as reduce stress.

Hypnotherapy

This is the use and application of hypnosis as a type of psychotherapy. It is employed as a technique to help a subject or patient through disturbing complications that are hounding them, particularly when other tactics of self-control cannot be relied on. Licensed physicians and psychologists may conduct a form of hypnotherapy on patients who are willing to assist them in treating compulsive gambling, posttraumatic stress, sleep disorders, depression, eating disorders, and anxiety. It is as well possible to see a certified hypnotherapist to help an individual in treating complications like weight management as well as smoking cessation. When one goes to see a skilled hypnotherapist, it is significant to note that they are not physicians or psychologists hence he may just be able to help them reach the hypnotic state and not to cure their more severe illnesses. Hence, it is important for an individual to ensure that whomever you approach has been certified to offer them with the hypnotic services, whether it is a physician or a hypnotherapist.

In the modern industry, the hypnotherapy process can be seen in numerous forms. All these forms have had varying levels of success based on the complication faced and the subjects. Below are some of the types that have been employed so Far.:

·   Ericksonian hypnotherapy.

·   Hypnotherapy to help reduce addictions.

·   Hypnotherapy to help in pain control/management in individuals suffering from chronic pain.

·   Hypnotherapy to help with habit control.

·   Hypnotherapy to help in the psychological therapy that subject is already undergoing.

- Hypnotherapy to help in relaxation.

- Hypnotherapy to help in eradicating skin diseases.

- Hypnosis to help in dealing with fears and phobias.

- Hypnotherapy to aid in soothing anxious patients about to undergo surgery.

- Hypnotherapy to help to check an athlete's performance before a competition.

- Hypnoanalysis— which is also referred to as age regression hypnotherapy.

- Hypnotherapy to help in weight loss.

- Cognitive-behavioral hypnotherapy—a blend of elements of the Cognitive Behavioral Therapy along with clinical hypnosis.

Military applications

Besides helping people with numerous health complications and addictions, human beings have wondered and speculated if hypnosis can be used by the government officials and the military to change the citizen's way of thinking about things. To date, there is little evidence that the American military has used or can use hypnosis to attain their objectives. In fact, a released document from the Freedom of Information Act archive lately showed that the hypnosis process has been examined for its use in martial/military applications

Regardless of the investigation that was done, the study deduced that there really was not any evidence to show that the hypnosis process would be suitable to use in a military application. Furthermore, there was not any proof that clearly indicated that hypnosis exists as a real phenomenon outside of the participant's expectancy, ordinary suggestion, and high motivation. The document additionally explains how it is nearly impossible for one to use hypnosis in a military/martial application. It stipulates, "Using hypnosis in surveillance is likely to bring about certain technical difficulties that haven't been come across in the laboratory or clinic. To get compliance from a resilient source, for instance, it is essential to hypnotize the cause under fundamentally hostile conditions.

There is not enough proof, experimental or clinical, that this is doable." The document explains further that it has been problematic to research on the applications and impact of hypnosis to be employed in the military as there is no individual who can state with finality whether hypnosis is an exclusive state with some accustomed responses or it is just a form of suggestion which has induced as an outcome of the rapport between the hypnotist and the subject.

Chapter 6.Brainwashing

Brainwashing is a tactic that we hear often. We are told that television commercials bombard us with what to buy, and we are exposed to people's rants on television, radio, the newspaper, online, and social media. These rants tell us what we should look like, what we should be eating, reading, voting for, wearing, etc. We are all subjected to the art of brainwashing on a daily basis and the amount of brainwashing continues to grow.

Before the creation of social media, we were still exposed to social media. However, they would only market to their target audience. If they weren't meant for you, they would be ignored until the following commercial or show came back on the air. For example, you wouldn't have paid much attention to a Polly Pocket or Barbie commercial unless you were a ten-year-old girl or someone who might buy the product for their child.

But things are not like that anymore. Advertising has moved past gender roles, and with the inception of social media, advertisements are now personally geared for us. These websites take information that we provide them. For instance, Facebook uses our likes, comments, status updates, etc. to find the perfect things to advertise to us. They are utilizing brainwashing techniques in the 21st century.

The History of Brainwashing

The term first appeared in the 1950s when Americans were deathly afraid of the spread of communism like it was a poisonous disease. This was the time of the Korean war and there was an extreme belief that Chines

Communists had found a way to mysteriously and effectively change the behavior of their prisoners of war.

However, most of the time when we in the modern world hear about brainwashing, we often think about religious cult groups. These groups take people from their families and isolate them, deprive them of sleep, and expose them to loud and repetitive chanting and singing. It didn't seem like there was a lot of torture involved in this type of brainwashing. Rather their minds were controlled by love and what they thought they were receiving from these groups which are things they were not receiving back at home.

Psychologists refer to brainwashing as thought reform, which falls in the category of social influence. In these instances, the brainwasher must have complete control over those who they are brainwashing. That means that all of the brainwasher's patterns: eating, sleeping, using the bathroom, and other human needs are based on the will of the brainwasher. The brainwasher has a process that they have to complete to make sure that they have exerted ultimate control. They break down their victim's identity so that they do not have one anymore. They then slowly replace the old identity with a whole new set of behaviors, attitudes, and beliefs that work in their new environment.

Brainwashing Techniques

During the Korean War, the American POWs went under a series of attacks on their sense of self, which is what changed their identity and their personal beliefs. This is the process that they experienced:

- Assault on identity – This is an attack on everything that the person thinks they are and their belief system. The brainwasher keeps denying everything that the victim is and attacks them for days, weeks, months and even years until they break down from exhaustion, confusion, and disorientation. At this point, they start to wonder if what they thought about themselves is even true.

- Guilt – They make the victim feel remorse for anything they had done big or small. Anything that the victim believes is criticized, to how they eat, what they are wearing, and how they look. This makes them feel a huge sense of shame about themselves to the point that whatever they do is wrong.

- Self-betrayal- Now that they question who they are, and they feel extremely guilty, the brainwasher will have the victim agree that they are a bad person. The brainwasher forces the victim to deny his friends, family, and peers who share the same views as them; through physical and/or mental force. The actual action of betrayal to the people that they once felt loyal too, magnifies their sense of shame, as well as their loss of identity.

- Breaking Point – The victim starts to have an identity crisis that reaches their mental breaking point. They start to question who they are, and what they are supposed to do. The victim could start losing their hold on reality because they do not understand who they are anymore and what is happening to them. This is when the brainwasher steps in and starts to tempt them with a new identity and belief system that will end their misery.

- Leniency – The following step in the process is called leniency, which is a sense of salvation. Now that the victim is in crisis mode, the brainwasher comes in and offers a sort of reprieve, kindness from the suffering and abuse that they have been facing. They might offer something to eat or drink, ask about their home and what they might miss. This seems huge at this point because of all they have suffered. The victim starts to feel a sense of relief, and even appreciation for their offering.

- Compulsion to Confess – This is when the brainwasher turns the manipulation around and tells the victim that they are the ones who can help themselves. This is a time where the victim is faced with not only the guilt of pain of their identity crisis, but they also feel the relief of the leniency that was offered by the brainwasher. Now, they start feeling a desire to return the kindness that was just offered them, and they start to think of the possibility of confessing their sins to relieve some of the pain and guilt they feel about themselves.

- Channeling of Guilt – After going through months of assault that has led to confusion, personal breakdown and moments of leniency from the brainwasher(s), the victim feels guilt, but they do not know what it is for. This is where the brainwasher comes in to remind them of what they have done wrong and connects the guilt to the victim's old belief system. This is where they are led to believe that the new belief system is something good and all of the pain, and agony is related to the old belief that they are holding on too.

- Releasing of Guilt – The victim now knows that there is a chance they can release their guilt. They attribute their guilt to the old belief system, and they can escape the guilt. All they need to do is denounce all of the people and institutions that are associated with their old identity and belief system. Then they can release all of their pain. Once the victim rejects all of his old self, this is when the brainwasher comes in to offer them the new belief system and identity to follow.

- Progress and Harmony – Now the brainwasher is there to help the victim rebuild themselves. The new identity and belief system are introduced as good. All of the abuse stops, and the victim is offered a sense of physical comfort and mental calm if they start believing the new system that was placed in front of them. However, the victim is given a choice or made to believe that they are given a choice to choose between their old self or possible new self. The new identity that they are being offered is safe because it not like the one which led to their breakdown.

- Final Confession and Rebirth – At this particular point in the process, the victim is ready to choose their new path, belief system, and identity. The old belief system is rejected because it does not offer the peace and security that they get with the new one. The victim is now inducted into the new system through a set of rituals or ceremonies because they are now reborn.

The process of brainwashing and mind control is not only devious, but it is dangerous and harmful to those who are involved. It is stripping them away from everything they are to further someone else's agenda. It can be scary to think that people can influence a person's mind that way.

Who Is Vulnerable to Brainwashing?

From 'The Manchurian Candidate,' a very prominent politician is held hostage by the Korean army during the war, and the senator is brainwashed into becoming a special agent for the Korean military, with the intention of assassinating the presidential contender. You can learn that even the most intelligent and powerful many can be easily brainwashed, but in the truth, the opposite is very likely.

This includes people that have:

- Been forced to live on the streets

- Lost their loved ones via death or divorce

- Been made redundant or sacked from their workplace

- Suffered or are suffering from an illness that they can't accept

How Can One Be Brainwashed?

A person who is attempting to brainwash you will want to know every detail about your life in order for them to manipulate your beliefs. The person will want to find out what your weakness, who you trust, is, and what your strengths are, who is vital to you, and who you listen to for advice.

After doing so, the person will begin the process of brainwashing, which will involve five steps:

Isolation

This is the first tactic towards brainwashing because when you have family and friends around you are harmful to the manipulators. The last thing that they desire is someone with a different idea as compared to their own, asking questions about what you are being asked to believe. This technique begins in the form of not allowing you to access to friends or family or constant checking where someone is and who they are with.

Attack on Self-Esteem

When a person wants to brainwash someone, the manipulators can only do so if their target is in a vulnerable condition and has a low level of self-confidence. A person who is broken is much easy to rebuild with the manipulator's beliefs.

The manipulator requires breaking down the target's self-esteem. This could be done through intimidation or embarrassment, physical abuse or verbal abuse, sleep deprivation. A manipulator will begin to regulate everything about the target's life, from the time they sleep to even using the washroom and from food.

Us Versus Them

For you to break down a person and reshape them in a different image, an alternative way of their livelihood must be introduced that is more attractive than the present livelihood.

Blind Obedience

This is the ultimate goal of a manipulator, where the target follows orders without question.

Chanting a similar statement over and over again is a good way of controlling a person. Not only is repeating the same statement a tip of calming the mind, but studies have shown that the analytical and the repetitive parts of the mind are not interchangeable. Meaning that you can only do one or the other, so how perfect for halting those doubting thoughts by chanting.

Monopolization of Perception

- The abuser utter things that causes you to be introspective, you look deeper, to solve issues of your soul.

- The abuser keeps your attention on them

- The manipulator makes it not possible for you to do things that are off-limits

- The abusers try to remove anything from you that they can't control.

Induced Exhaustion

Brainwashers try to weaken your capability to resist their control by:

- Finding tactics to make you feel guilty for not agreeing to their demands.

- Keeping you often busy meeting their very high standards of holiness, parenting, and cleanliness

- Claim your character is sub-par and they insist that you correct it

- Demand that your friends with their boss's spouse, attend social events that improve their professional career

- Add tasks to your life that are beyond and above what is often expected in a normal relationship.

Threats

The brainwasher threatens to leave you. The threats are credible to you. The abusers deliver the threats via body language too.

Degradation

The brainwasher harms you more when you resist their demands or question their ideas and stand up for your right. Any moment that your anger rises, the manipulator must deal with your fury, the punishment is more severe than if you just did the damn thing, to begin with.

The brainwasher will tend to degrade you with mere words, via physical or sexual abuse and humiliate you in the presence of their coworkers or friends at any time. The humiliation tears down your sense of self-worth to a lower level.

Demonstrating Omnipotence

Most Brainwashers will stalk you during relationships, use their friends, or they will exploit lucky coincidence to prove that they know everything you do even when they are not present.

Testing

Brainwashers can never think of their work as accomplished, as there are often situations where the target could begin to regain control of their own autonomy and begin thinking critically for themselves again. Testing their targets not only shows that they are still brainwashed, but it allows the brainwasher to see just how much control he/she still has over his/her targets. The test could involve doing a criminal act, for example, burglarizing a home or robbing a store.

Chapter 7.How Brainwashing Can Be a Part of Dark Psychology

Brainwashing is going to be the slow process of taking the ideas that a victim has about their identity and their beliefs and then replacing these with new ideas, ones that are going to suit the purpose of the manipulator. Brainwashing can occur in a narrow and a wide context. For example, a brainwasher could use the techniques in order to control one person, or they could use those techniques in order to control the minds of a larger group all at once.

The Process of Brainwashing

The starting point of brainwashing is going to be the social circumstances and the mental state of the victim. This is going to be the foundation for the rest of the process, and if the manipulator is not able to figure this part out, then the brainwashing session just won't be successful. Brainwashing is not a process that is going to work out for everyone. It is going to require a good identification of a person who is looking for something or someone who has a void they are trying to fill.

This brings us to an important point. Who is the ideal victim for a brainwasher? People who have had their existing reality shaken up because of some recent events are some great targets for brainwashers. If you have lost someone you are really close to or had another dramatic or traumatic event in your life, then you may be more susceptible to brainwashing.

Once the brainwasher has found their victim, either through the Internet or in person, the process of brainwashing is able to begin. Contrary to the popular image you may have in your mind about a brainwasher, this person is often going to come across as someone who is rational, friendly, and calm. Someone who seems to have their lives together in a way the victim wishes they could have their own. Imagine how it would feel if you were homeless and a celebrity you admired befriended you. This is often how the process of meeting the brainwasher is going to feel for the victim.

The brainwasher is going to get to work right away. The first step for them is to create a level of rapport and trust between them and the victim. This is going to be done with superficial and deep similarities. The superficial similarities could involve some surface level preferences, something like enjoying the same food or sport as the other person.

They will then move on to a deeper level of rapport, some that could involve a deeper shared experience that they had in the past. The brainwasher will most likely fake these, in a convincing manner, in order to create these bonds. So, if the victim shares with the brainwasher that they lost a close relative in the past, then the brainwasher is all of a sudden going to have a story that is similar to share with the victim.

This false connection and warmth emotionally are not the only thing that is going to occur. The brainwasher wants to cement that new bond as quickly as possible. It is not uncommon for them to provide favors and gifts to their victim. They could send then a gadget or some other item they may find useful. They may treat the victim to a meal. The point of doing this is to create a sense of gratitude and indebtedness from the victim to that brainwasher. This is going to soften up a lot of the resistance that the victim may experience.

After the resistance has been stripped away a little bit, the following step is going to be a sort of utopian presentation. This is going to involve the brainwasher slowly and increasingly offering a solution to any and all problems that the victim previously opened up about. This is not going to be a big hard push or sell. Rather, the brainwasher knows how to do this in an offhand and casual way to make sure they don't deal with any negative experiences by pressing the victim. This solution is always going to be the personality, ideology, or cult that the brainwasher is working to make the victim convert too.

When these steps are done properly, the initial stages that we have mentioned are going to leave the victim wanting more. The victim is going to want more information and more understanding of the solution that the brainwasher hints at. The brainwasher may even withhold some of this information in the beginning, treating it as something that the victim needs to do some work to attain. The point of doing this is to push some motivation on the victim in order to seek out and accept the information they are eventually going to hear.

After the victim has had some time being spoon-fed snippets of this belief system, and they have shown they will respond well to them, the brainwasher is going to be careful in order to reveal the right information at the right time. This is a concept that is called a gradual revelation or milk before meat. It is basically going to include the presentation of an easy to accept idea before the really controversial idea is revealed.

For example, if the brainwasher is trying to convert the victim over to religious terrorism, they would not just start out with the terrorism part. They may initially start focusing on the fact that God loves the victim, something that the victim is likely to accept. The more objectionable ideas, such as. Once the victim has accepted that last part, then this brainwashing session is at a point of no return.

At this point, you may be curious as to why the victim is still engaging with the brainwasher, especially when these more objectionable ideas start to become apparent. There are three main reasons:

- The vulnerable victim has been worked on by the brainwasher. They feel a strong sense of liking the brainwasher, and they want to get the approval of the brainwasher.

- The victim has invested some time, and in some cases, money, in the process up to this point. This is often known as the sunk cost fallacy. The victim is going to feel like it is a bad idea to throw away all the hard work and money they have put into the process as well.

- During this process, the brainwasher has been amassing a lot of sensitive and secretive information on the victim. The brainwasher is often willing to hold this information over the victim to keep the victim on the right path.

The Impact of Brainwashing

The above analysis that we did about the process of brainwashing is going to show how severe this technique can be. It is basically changing the beliefs and the inner identity of the victim, and this can be a big deal. Sure, the manipulator is going to get what they want out of the process, but the victim is going to lose out on their real identity and often gets so far into the process that they aren't sure what went wrong.

There are a lot of different impacts that will come with brainwashing after the process is completed. The first one is a loss of identity. A feature of many ideologies and cults is that the people who go through the initiation process are given a new name. This helps the psyche of the person to completely detach from whatever their old identity is. They can believe things and even do things they never would have done in the past because that old person they were no longer exists. When this process is carried out the proper way, it can leave a victim feeling like all the parts of their old identity are no longer real or permanent and that they have woken up from a nightmare.

Post-traumatic stress disorder, or PTSD, can sometimes be a hallmark of those who managed to escape or who are rescued from a situation where they were brainwashed. The victims of these brainwashing endeavors are going to show some of the same psychological and physical signs as war veterans who were right in the battle. The severity of this traumatic aftermath shows that this type of process, of the manipulator getting more control over the victim, could harm the victim as much as if they went to war.

Brainwashing is something that can have a lasting impact. There are plenty of examples of individuals who were rescued, or who managed to escape, from their brainwashing situation, who then went back to that situation of their own free will. Even when they were able to leave the brainwashing and controlling environment they were in, the legacy that came with that process was done so well and runs so deep in their mind that the victim actually wants to return to it. This just shows the power of using this brainwashing process and how much a manipulator could gain when using this kind of process.

Chapter 8.Advanced Dark Psychology and Manipulation Techniques

We are going to be taking a look at some advanced dark psychology and manipulation techniques. These techniques are highly effective and are generally regarded as favorites for well-versed manipulators. If you happen to fall into one of these traps, you'll be surprised at the level of sophistication which is attached to them. Moreover, some manipulators may be so good that you will hardly notice that you have fallen into such traps.

If you are entertaining the possibility of using these techniques for your own benefit, please be advised that utilizing dark psychology tactics such as these may get you what you want, but the cost to others may be quite high. So, you do need to be prepared to face the consequences should others be potentially harmed in this situation.

In addition, these techniques do take some time to perfect and develop as they require a good degree of skill and experience. That being said, your ability to make the most of the dark psychology tactics in the pursuit of your personal goals may lead you to gain deeper insights into the world of human psychology and how the human psyche works.

Gaslighting

This technique has a bit of an unusual name, but its overall effectiveness is remarkable. Its effectiveness lies is getting people to question their own perception of reality. As such, gaslighting consists of manipulating the victim into believing what the manipulator wants them to believe even when there is clear evidence against what the manipulator is saying.

The classic example of gaslighting can be seen in cases of abuse. The abuser repeatedly tells the victim that there is no such abuse happening even when it's clear that the victim has been abused in some manner. This type of denial forces the victim to question their own perception of the events that have taken place. When effective, the victim may not necessarily accept what the manipulator has said, but rather, will question their own perception to the degree that they have no way of differentiating abuse from non-abuse situations.

Gaslighting is commonly used by politicians. This is why their first reaction is to deny everything when a scandal break. 9 times out of 10, politicians get away with initial denials. Unless the media decides to dig deeper and produce compelling evidence supporting claims, politicians will simply stonewall everything. This is intended to get voters to question the media's accuracy. The intent is not to convince the public they have done no wrong; the intent is to generate enough confusion to where the public gives politicians the benefit of the doubt even when they are clearly guilty.

Reverse Psychology

This technique is one of the classics in the world of manipulation. It generally consists of telling someone the opposite of what you want them to do or know. The way this works is that people will generally respond to what they shouldn't do rather than what they should. For instance, when you tell a child not to do something, that is the first thing they do. This type of response persists throughout a person's life. When individuals are told that they should not believe one thing or the other, they will pay closer attention to it.

Consider this situation:

You are looking to force your employees to work overtime without questioning it. However, getting them to actually log the hours can be really challenging as no one is keen on staying beyond their usual shift. So, you really can't do much to convince them to work overtime.

Then, you get an idea: why not ban overtime? That is, anyone who wants to work overtime cannot do so. The justification behind it is that since no one wants to stay longer hours, then there will be no overtime. In fact, you could take it a step further and hire temp workers to fill in the extra hours. Now, your regular staff is concerned that others are encroaching upon their jobs. In the end, you may get resistance from your usual staff who are now demanding to work overtime in order to get rid of the temp workers.

In the end, you have successfully manipulated your staff to work overtime. You were able to play with their sense of security by banning overtime and then bringing other workers to cover the hours they wouldn't.

A convention playbook would have sought to incentivize workers so they would be more willing to stay longer hours. But this would have meant paying more or offering greater benefits. In the end, your manipulation attempts were successful without conceding any additional benefits.

Good Cop, Bad Cop

This technique alludes to the common movie plot in which two detectives question a suspect in a variety of ways. However, the technique takes shape when one cop is overly aggressive while the other is more condescending and friendlier.

What you see in this case is not a struggle between various types of personality. What you are seeing is a clear attempt at confusing the suspect. You see, when you are faced with an overly aggressive person, your natural instinct is to go into a defensive position. Then, when you are immediately confronted by a "nice" person, your psyche is thrown out of whack. You really don't know how to react. You may be fearful or suspicious.

The same goes for cases in which you're dealing with a kind person and then you are suddenly confronted by an aggressive individual. When this occurs, the shock that occurs in your mind may be enough to get you into a state of panic.

Depending on how mentally tough someone is, they may break down and hold out for a longer period of time. In some more extreme cases, interrogators may resort to torture tactics in order to extract information from a suspect. While this is illegal in a criminal case, it is commonly used in the underworld of espionage.

To play this game with people, all you need to do is keep them off balance. While this doesn't mean that you should be moody, it means that you shouldn't be predictable. Otherwise, people around you will know what pushes your buttons and then choose to use that against you. That's why you need to measure your reactions and use them to suit your goals. If you feel that being nice will get you ahead, then be nice. But if you feel that you need to make an example out of someone, then you may have no other choice.

Half-Truths

This technique is the kind that you really need to think through. Half-truths are all about mixing lies with the truth. This is why you need to think things through. If you just blurt out lies without actually thinking about them, then you are liable to make a mistake. If you do, then you'll get caught and your cover will be blown.

In order for this technique to be effective, you need to mix lies in such a way that they make sense with scrutinized and contrasted with the truth. They need to be credible and presented in a manner that makes sense to those who will hear them. Often, manipulators add or omit details that are convenient to them. So, the information is true, on the whole, but the details of the truth are twisted to suit your benefit. As the saying goes, "the devil is in the details."

A good means of implementing half-truths is through rumors. Nowadays, social media is a great way of spreading rumors. In fact, it is so effective that you don't really need to get people to believe it; all you need is to sow a seed of doubt. As long as you can get people to doubt the accuracy of the information, or partially accept its validity, then you have done your job. By the time the affected parties seek to restore their reputations or set the record straight, it will have been too late. That is why you need to strike first and often. That way, the victim will have no choice but to go into crisis mode.

If you fear such an attack on yourself, then you need to hit the manipulator back where it will hurt them. You need to discredit them at all costs. That will sow the seed of doubt on the source of the information and give you a fighting chance to defend yourself.

Lying

This technique is definitely the most advanced of the lot. If you are going to flat out lie, then you need to be very convincing. Often, this may include building a brand-new persona for yourself or embellishing accomplishment which may, or may not, have actually happened.

When you lie, you need it to be credible and logical. You can't expect people to believe outrageous claims unless your victims are incredibly gullible and/or ignorant. Depending on who you're dealing with, you may be able to get away with more or less.

For instance, if you are dealing with a highly educated group of people, any claims you make need to stand up to scrutiny. Otherwise, you'll be questioned to a point where you won't be able to recover. However, if you do your homework, you'll be ready for any questioning.

In this case, think about con artists and fraudsters. They are able to build up lies that are so complex that the average person won't be able to question them. Since the devil is in the detail, lies need to be intricately built as possible. That will give greater credence to your hoax. However, any good lie starts off from the truth. That is what lays the foundation for a credible lie.

The most important thing to keep in mind is that you need to be consistent. The front needs to be the same for anyone you come into contact with. Otherwise, switching versions on people will invariably lead you to slip up and get caught in your own lie.

Chapter 9.Reading Micro-Expressions and Body Language

With the nitty-gritty details about dark psychology, manipulators, and the dark triad out of the way, it is time to get to some skills you will be able to utilize. The first and most important skill that will be at the foundation of everything, is the ability to read and recognize the feelings and general comfort of those around you.

Expressions

Body language is surprisingly universal—while several cultures will have their own unique gestures and readings of gestures, there are several types of body language that mean the same things across cultures and oceans. This may be, in part, due to the fact that humans have seven basic emotions that are believed to be at the root of all feelings that can be felt. These seven emotions are perhaps the most simplified versions of what is being felt, each encompassing a wide range of different emotions that can be felt by humans. Each of the emotions that will be listed here will describe facial expressions associated with them.

Happiness

Happiness is often characterized by two identifying factors on the face—the eyes should be crinkled, with a wrinkle at the corners that is almost impossible to fake, and by a smile, either wide or small.

Sadness

Sadness is characterized, namely by drawing eyebrows together. They are pulled together, with the innermost corners shifting upwards and causing wrinkles in between them. Along with these distinctive eyebrows, which are incredibly difficult to replicate without genuine feeling, oftentimes, the mouth is pulled downward into a frown with the bottom lip pouting outward.

Fear/Anxiety

In response to anxiety or fear, people typically raise their eyebrows, with the arch relatively straight. The forehead will show wrinkles between the brows as well. The eyes are usually widened, with the whites of the eyes being visible above the iris, and the pupils are usually dilated as well. This dilation of pupils is impossible to mimic, occurring entirely unconsciously. Oftentimes, the mouth is open as well, with the lips slightly parted and tensed.

Contempt

In contempt, the expression is actually almost entirely neutral. The only exception is a slight raise of one corner of the mouth for a moment during a hard stare, as if flashing a smirk.

Disgust

When someone feels disgusted, they look at it with lowered brows and pinched, raised eyelids. Usually, the nose wrinkles backward with the nostrils flared out, and the upper lip rises up, flashing teeth. This essentially shields the sensitive parts of the body—the eyes and nose are protected from whatever disgusting thing has caused such a strong reaction.

Anger

Anger typically involves lowered brows that hood the eyes, their brows coming together in the middle and creating a wrinkled forehead. Their eyes are usually staring without blinking in a harsh, hostile glare, and lips are tense.

Surprise

Surprise is usually noticeable by someone exhibiting raised eyebrows, with the arch nice and rounded. The upper part of the forehead is usually wrinkled as well, and the eyes are wide, with the whites being visible around the entire iris. The mouth may also be hung loosely open.

Facial Body Language

Beyond those most common emotional expressions, it is important to understand whether individual movements of the face are good or bad, as well as what they are implying. Take a look at the eyebrows, eyes, and mouth, and learn the most telling positions and movements they take unconsciously. Keep in mind, however, that when people are trying to hide deceit, they often control their face. It is not always the most reliable source of expressions or honesty, although it can be useful.

Eyebrows

- Lowering the brows: When you encounter someone with lowered brows, oftentimes, they are showing that what they want more than anything else is to not be engaged in whatever is happening. Whether angry, stuck in a confrontation, or disgusted, the connotation is almost always negative. It is also a telltale sign of deceit, especially when the person lowers their head in conjunction with lowering their brows.

- Raising the brows: Raising brows, on the other hand, shows increased attention or a sort of emphasis. It is seen in surprise when something suddenly and unexpectedly draws one's attention, and it can also be seen in people who are showing attraction in someone else.

- One brow raised: When one brow is raised, it usually shows disbelief or dubiousness at what was just said. It almost always brings along a connotation of not believing whatever was just said, or that someone disagrees with you. A quick twitch of one brow can also be seen in contempt sometimes.

- Knitting brows together: When the brows come together, they also create creases between them. It can be seen in negative, stressed emotions such as sadness, worry, and confusion.

- Lowering the middle of the brows: Typically, lowering the middle of the brows, creating a straight line rather than any real arch implies a frustration or anger being felt.

- Raising the middle of the brows: When the middle of the brows is raised, on the other hand, it usually shows either surprise, fear, or even relief. Because of the contradictory nature of some of the meanings to this expression, you should take it in conjunction with some other body language as well to be sure of the meaning.

Eyes

The eyes can communicate more than people would be likely to expect—after all, all they do is roll around to direct gaze, right?

Wrong.

They are also used to make and hold eye contact, the pupils can dilate and constrict, and even the frequency at which you blink can be telling of what is happening in your mind at any given moment.

- Direction of gaze: Interestingly enough, even the direction you look can be telling as to what is happening within your mind. When you look at someone or something, it is because you are interested in it. Especially if you notice that someone's gaze is repeatedly returning to the same thing over and over again, you have a likely sign that they are interested in something that is not you or your conversation. For example, looking constantly at another person implies that the individual would rather go speak to that other person, or looking at a drink implies that the person wants it. This can even go one step further—the direction your eyes turn when asked a question while you think can also decipher whether you are truthful. When you look to the left, you are utilizing the parts of your brain that recall memories. When you look to the right, you utilize the part of your brain used for creation and fiction, implying the creation of lies. When you look down, however, you appear to be shameful, and people often assume you are lying.

- Intensity of gaze: Have you noticed how some people can just stare you down with an unwavering gaze, but it makes you uncomfortable? Or how others may struggle to make eye contact with you at all, constantly looking away from you instead? The intensity of the gaze and how often you spend making eye contact tells how comfortable you are. The most natural, comfortable eye contact that implies that you are welcome and encouraged to continue speaking involves occasional glances away from the eyes but returning to continue eye contact shortly after. Too much eye contact is aggressive, confrontational, and unnerving. Too little shows shame, fear, or deception.

- Frequency of blinking: Along with the intensity of your gaze, people tend to look at how often you blink when you are making eye contact. Those who do not blink when making eye contact come across as far more aggressive than those who blink at a normal rate. Blinking too much, however, implies that you are flustered or stressed out. The rate of blinking can also allow you to identify when someone is lying—during the process of lying, oftentimes individuals do not blink at all while telling a lie, but immediately afterward, blink more often than usual.

- Pupil dilation: Pupil dilation is also important to understand, even though in most instances, you are not likely to be close enough to recognize the tiny shifts in levels. However, pupil dilations are impossible to fake, making them incredibly reliable. Typically, the pupils will dilate in response to something attractive, something surprising, something frightening, or when someone is lost in intensive thought—the more dilated the pupil, the more intense the thought.

Mouth

The mouth also can provide some pretty useful information if you direct your attention to it, and not just through verbal communication—the way that the mouth moves, whether open or shut, tense or relaxed, or even with the other person touching their mouth, can tell more of the story than the words ever will.

- Lips are relaxed: When the lips are relaxed, the person is usually relaxed. They are likely confident, comfortable, and in control of the situation without any worry or stress.

- Lips are parted: Usually, when the lips are parted, the individual is flirting with the other person. However, it is also used when one person is trying to get the attention of another, typically in the context of wanting the person to stop talking so they can speak as well.

- Teeth are borne: When someone bares their teeth, they are either smiling, which is positive, or snarling, which shows that the other person is feeling intense anger or aggression.

- Lips are twitching: When the lips are twitching, particularly on one side, it shows either contempt or an attempt to hide one's feelings. Usually, the twitch was the uncontrollable impulse to do something, but the person overrode that impulse, leaving behind only a nearly imperceptible twitch of the lip in its wake.

- Touching the mouth or biting the fingers: When someone is touching their mouth or biting their fingers, they are either under stress and attempting to self-soothe, or they are hiding something from you.

- Biting the cheek or the lip: Oftentimes, biting the cheek or lip also implies that the other person is nervous, afraid, unsure how to react, or is attempting to hold back a true reaction.

Body Language

Beyond facial features, the body itself is just as expressive. The way the body moves can tell you a surprising amount of details about what is happening within the other person's mind, ranging from feeling entirely uncomfortable with an interaction, to feeling confident, in control, and powerful. Keep in mind that some people may express themselves in different ways and that this suggestion should be approached as a guide and not a guarantee to help you identify any emotions in anyone else.

Head

The first part of the body you will learn about will be the head. The head, beyond expressions and facial features, can be moved in a wide variety of ways that can also help provide insight into the mind of another.

- Tilt: People naturally direct their head toward those they feel a rapport, or connection, with. Even when that person is not necessarily talking in a group, people will unconsciously tilt their heads toward the leader of the group. It can also tilt toward someone that they feel a connection with. Conversely, tilting the head back, away from someone, implies distrust, suspicion, or being unsure in general. By tilting the head to the side, an individual encourages the other person to continue speaking.

- Nod: When someone nods, it is usually a sign of affirmation, confirming the agreement, or confirming that the individual is listening. When someone nods quicker, it means they are growing impatient and want to disengage but feel too polite to do so. When the nodding is slower and more thoughtful, it implies that the other person is still actively listening and engaged in the conversation.

- Watch the chin: The chin, like the tilt of the head, can show a lot. When the chin is raised upwards, the neck is exposed. This is a sign of arrogance—it is essentially daring the other person to even try touching them or hurting them. When it is tucked downward, shielding the neck, however, it shows a level of insecurity.

Arms/shoulders

The way the arms are held can also be incredibly revealing. Take a look at some of the most common ways that arms are held and what they mean:

- Arms pulled backward: When the arms are drawn backward, it is usually because the individual feels uncomfortable or defensive. In drawing backward, they are able to make their arms less available to grab—as the shoulders move away, they are less readily available during an attack.

- Arms expanded: The arms can be expanded outward, relaxed at the shoulders and allowed to hang naturally. This is a sign of openness and comfort, implying that the other person is comfortable with what is happening at the moment.

- Arms drawn inward: Conversely to expanding the arms, when the arms are pulled inward, the individual is seen as making him or herself smaller and therefore less of a target. It implies insecurity or discomfort.

- Arms entirely still: When the arms are entirely still at the sides, they typically look quite unnatural, and for a good reason—usually the other person is trying to control their arms to avoid exposing any body language that could be taken advantage of. This can go one step further as well, with one arm crossing the body so one hand can hold the other arm still as if physically restraining it. This is a tell for lying as well, as the individual is literally holding him or herself back.

- Arms crossed: Arms crossed is often seen as the ultimate form of defensiveness—usually the individual feels incredibly uncomfortable with whatever is happening and is literally shielding his vulnerable chest—protecting the vital organs within his ribcage from attack.

- Arms raised upwards: Sometimes, arms are thrown upwards, above the shoulder lines. Usually, this is in some sort of emphasis—either in joy, surprise, or even confusion.

Hands

Like the arms, the hands are also incredibly expressive. Because they can be moved in so many different ways, they can be used to show a wide range of different feelings and mental states.

- Hands-on hips: Hands on the hips may often come across as aggressive or intimidating, but it is actually meant to be a power pose—it instills confidence and implies a readiness to act.

- Palms upward: When palms are turned upwards, it typically implies someone is trying to be seen as trustworthy, worth listening to, and is speaking earnestly.

- Palms downward: When the palms are downwards, however, it conveys dominance and control—this is often seen in politics. People or leaders will put their hands outward to signify that they have control of the situation. They may also punctuate their words with a few chopping motions downwards, essentially forcing the point they are trying to get across.

- Hands behind back: Hand behind the back can happen in several different ways—the hands can be relaxed, with one hand resting in the palm of the other, or it could involve one hand holding onto the wrist or arm of the other. When the hands are resting together, it implies dominance, control, and authority. It is calm and collected. When the hand is gripping the other hand, however, it implies that the other person is attempting to control himself. The higher the handgrips, the more out of control that person feels in that particular moment.

- Hands in pockets: Oftentimes, this is seen as deceptive, or maybe done out of anxiety as well.

- Steepling: Steepling involves the palms facing each other but never touching, and the fingertips of both hands resting against each other. When this happens, the other person is showing that they are confident, in control, and that they are powerful.

- Clenched fists: When fists are clenched, usually the other person is attempting to exert control over themselves—they may feel stressed or out of control and be trying to get it back. They may also be feeling extreme anger, frustration, or aggression.

- Rubbing hands together: When the hands rub together, a person is signifying that he or she is anticipating something and is excited about whatever will come after.

- Pointing: Pointing is often considered quite aggressive and dominant, much like a parent scolding his or her children. It can be accentuated by someone turning the point into a jab.

- Hands-on heart: When someone places a hand or hands on the heart, they are typically attempting to show that they are speaking from the heart. Of course, this is incredibly easy to falsify, so keep in mind that the other person may not be being as honest as they are attempting to imply.

- Tapping fingers: When the person is tapping their fingers along their arm, desk, or any other surface, the other person is trying to signal that they are impatient and would like the conversation or interaction to wrap up as quickly as possible.

Legs/feet

The last part of the body you will look at is the legs, and the feet attached to them. These parts of the body are typically forgotten by those who are attempting to disguise their body language, and because of that, it is a great baseline to identify true intentions. The mouth may lie, but the feet tell the truth. When you are talking to someone and are unsure about what the other person is thinking at the moment, try looking at their feet—you will likely get some valuable information.

- Crossed legs: This can show dominance, so long as you do it with an ankle over a knee. Of course, that is largely a male position. When the legs are crossed over the knees, particularly with women, it shows flirtation. When the legs are crossed at the ankles, it shows that you are anxious, afraid, or uncertain.

- Sitting with legs spread: This shows that you are marking an area as your own—you are showing that you are dominant over it and not afraid to fight someone for it.

- Pointing feet toward the speaker: When the feet are pointing toward the speaker, it is a good sign that the listeners are incredibly engaged in the conversation. They may be interested in the speaker as a person, or in whatever is being said. Regardless, this is a good sign, and the conversation is encouraged to continue.

- Pointing feet away from the speaker: When you notice that the other person is pointing their feet away, however, there is a high likelihood that the other person is disengaged from the speaker. They may be interested in something else more, such as leaving or going to speak to someone else. Check to see where the person's feet are pointing if you want to understand what it is that they want at that moment.

- Toes pointed up: When toes point upwards as if the person has shifted their stance slightly, so their heel is rolled back and toes go upward, the person is likely relaxed and enjoying any interaction that is happening at that moment. Check to see if they are showing other signs of relaxation as well—you'll likely find a smile and relaxed arms.

- Bouncing on feet: Much like a child literally jumping in the air in joy or excitement, adults will also bounce a bit—usually, they tone down the behavior, so they are not seen as childish, but you can notice a shift in their feet.

Tapping feet: If the other person is tapping their feet, but there is no music playing, chances are the other person is not interested in what is happening. It can show signs of anxiety, impatience, or disinterest and wanting to leave

Chapter 10.Case Studies

Below we look at some baffling cases that have prominently put to the fore the mystery of dark psychology. What we notice is that the worst of human traits, the darkness that lives in all of us, come out during experiments. And not just in the subjects. Even the ones experimenting showed great inhumanity.

Scientific Experiments

The scientist has conducted experiments on people for as long as science and experiments and hypotheses have existed. Yet, there was a strange twist. It was a twist, perhaps more twisted than the entire subversives of dark psychology. Scientists have also been in the fore in proving the dark psychology as they attempted to find out about something else. So traumatizing were these experiments that some of the participants' permanent psychological issues. Most of them involved manipulating test subjects to get them to perform, which you will realize as one of the dark personality traits - Machiavellian.

In the 1960s, a doctor came to light after it emerged that she used electroshock therapy on children. The horror didn't start there, as, during the interview process, she would select her patients by having a parent bring their child, where she would press their heads. Any slight movement and she would declare the child had schizophrenia. And during the shock, she never showed sympathy on the children, with her youngest being just three years.

Then, from 53-73, the government of the US embarked on experiments that would help them find out how to manipulate people. The project was called MKUltra. These experiments involved subjecting people without their knowledge, to drugs that altered their brains, hypnosis, sexual abuse, and many other forms of torture. This experiment just gave a glimpse of the murk that was human psychology. Subjecting innocent people to such cruelty in the name of the research was itself peak dark psychology.

The most famous experiment in psychology was the Stanford Experiment, which aimed to find out the cause of conflict between the prisoners and their guards. The scientist selected twenty-four prisoners and assigned them roles of either guards or prisoners. Then they were awarded a model prison within the premises. What emerged was that the prisoners playing guards were so strict and so extreme in their torture of the prisoners that the scientists stopped the experiment after just six days! Sick.

The Milgram experiment was also another that put to the fore the repressed terrible recesses of human psychology. In 1961, Stanley Milgram, a Yale University Psychologist, set out to find just why Eichmann and other millions of soldiers in the Holocaust just followed orders. This was a quarter a year after Eichmann had gone to trial. Two people were placed in separate rooms but could hear each other. The experiment was to see the willingness of someone to follow authority orders. Between these two participants, one was an actor. The test subject would then read the question to the actor, and if the actor answered any of them wrongly, the test subject would administer an electric shock to the actor. Nearly every single test subject continued pressing the electric shock button when the experimenter to them that they would not be held personally responsible for their actions.

Another case was of David Peter Reimer, who was born biologically male. When he was just seven months, he suffered a damaging injury to his manhood as someone circumcised him. John Money, a psychologist and a great believer in gender as something that one learns, convinced David's parents that their son would more likely be more functional as a girl. He must have been a Machiavellian. But while Money put his money on his idea is a success, David's account much contradicted Money's. David never identified as female, so that is where it all falls apart. David spent his childhood traumatized due to being teased and ostracized, leaving him depressed. Then, at just 38 years old, David couldn't take it anymore and committed suicide with a gunshot to the head.

Another example of the scientists being total monsters was in the Washington and Oregon prison testicle radiation experiment. Between 1963 and 1973, several inmates from these two prisons volunteered as test subjects in a trial that aimed to find the effects of radiation on testicles. One hundred thirty inmates were bribed with cash and promise of parole to take part in the experiment. Here, we see the dark part of the scientist come out. Manipulating prisoners into taking part in a dangerous operation is inhumane. The inmates agreed to take part in the experiment. The study was the brainchild of the government.

The scientists exposed some of the test subjects to massive doses of radiation. Now, exposure to radiation is dangerous, even when it is in small doses. Radiation rays have a permanent effect on the human cells, mutating the DNA and other cells in the body, leading to deformities. This affects not just the test subject, but the children will have as well. It took some time when the prisoners found out that they had not been told about the whole truth regarding the dangers of the experiment. They settled a $2.4 million agreement at the turn of the century.

Psychopaths - Serial Killers

Serial killers have, for a long time, held the fascination of many people. Their wanton disregard for necessary human conscience has forever baffled and intrigued not just the ordinary people, but the figures of authority, scientists, and psychologists.

If we had nothing to lose, would we be just as lethal? If the Milgram experiment above was anything to go by, perhaps we could be just as prone to violence as serial killers. But still, the lack of inhibition shown by these killers is legendary, a revelation of the darkness rolling just beneath our human conscience.

Ed Gein was a farmer in Plainfield, Wisconsin, notorious for robbing women's bodies from graves. He also was a murderer and often used parts of the women's remains to decorate his isolated farm in Wisconsin and make items on clothing. Gein was active between 1945-1957 and died in 1984 at a mental institution. He had so much impact that he was loosely used to create fictional killers.

Night Stalker

Richard Ramirez was a deranged murderer that came to be dubbed by the media as 'The Night Stalker.' In 14 months, Ramirez embraced the night as his accomplice, gravitating towards the embrace of the dark as he made a way through homes in a prowl that saw him leave behind 13 dead across California.

Before he made his first kill, the authority had arrested Ramirez for attempted rape, but the woman did not pursue the case, choosing not to testify against him. Let, free, Ramirez began a long murder spree that was violent, brutal, and callous. He often showed no remorse, and his first murder victim, 76-year old Jennie Vincow, on June 28th, 1984. Ramirez brutally raped then murdered the woman by slitting the throat so deep that she was almost decapitated.

During his trial, he gave little away in terms of remorse, and as he was led to prison to serve his life sentence. On his way to prison, he couldn't help but taunt the people gathered outside the court to witness his trial.

Ramirez had a difficult childhood, suffering two severe head injuries that left him suffering from frequent epileptic attacks. His father was abusive to him, leading to Ramirez running away from home. He found comfort in his cousin Miguel, a war veteran, who had developed a taste for torturing women in Vietnam. He showed Ramirez the photos of the torture and killed his wife as Ramirez watched. Miguel may have influenced Ramirez to develop a taste for blood.

Grim Sleeper

When women began disappearing at a neighborhood in Los Angeles, no one would have suspected the personable Loonie Frankline Jr. Neighbors and friends described him as someone willing to help and didn't display the usual traits of psychopathy, like being a loner.

Franklin earned his nickname due to the 14-year break he seemed to have taken between murdering his first eight victims between 1985-1988. He began again in 2002, though authorities believe that he may be responsible for more deaths than the eleven the court found him guilty of.

Franklin targeted women and with hundreds of polaroid photos of women, some of whom were his victims, others who were still alive. Others were never identified, which led authorities to suspect him of more deaths than what he was charged with.

Franklin shot his victims at close range and dumped them near trash cans and on alleyways. Often, he would target vulnerable women off the streets.

He was sentenced to death in August 2016, although authorities are still trying to connect him to 15 other killings.

Edmund Kemper

Kemper was a bright child who suffered a lot of abuse, physical and emotional, under his mother. He had also been displaying psychopathic tendencies as a child, often torturing and killing animals, which is observed in a big number of people who end up being psychotic killers.

He often decapitated his sister's dolls as a child and had once stalked his teacher in second grade outside her home with his father's bayonet. When he was ten, Kemper killed the family's cat. Then, he killed another when he was 13. This second time, he took up some parts of the animal and kept them in the cloth closet, where his mother came across them, much to her horror probably.

When he was 14, he left home to find his father in California. His determination to see his old man paid off, but rather than find comfort and the man rejected him. He had been belittled continuously by Kemper's mother, and this may have led him to hate the boy. Depressed and angry, he went to live with his grandparents, both of whom he shot dead in 1964, at just 15. He was then committed to Atascadero State Hospital for the criminally insane but was released back to his mother five years after, much to his chagrin.

He began fantasizing about killing his mother but decided first to perfect his murder skills.

Between 1972 and 1973, Kemper began his killing spree. Targeting female students, he would pick up those hitchhiking a ride on the road. But then, rather than take them to their destination, he took them out in the wild, where he killed them. Then, to further add to his derangement, he would have sex with the dead women, decapitate them and take their heads back to his apartment, where he would have sex with them too. Scary stuff this one.

Then, in 1973, on Good Friday, Kemper achieved what may have been his biggest goal—he murdered his mother. Taking a hammer, he bludgeoned her to death, then proceeded to strangle her friend. Afterward, he also defiled his mother's head.

After he was done, he made a phone call to the local police, where he confessed to them. They were initially reluctant to arrest him, as he was known to them, but they were down on him soon after he began revealing details of the murders that only the murderer would know. At this point, when they came to take him, he did not resist. He was just twenty-four at the time.

Alton Coleman And Debra Brown

The Bonnie and Clyde of the serial killer's horrific world, the two traversed across six states, leaving eight people dead in their wake.

At age 19, Coleman had already had six counts of rape charged against him. It was reported that Coleman had unusually strong sexual urges that he then took to satisfying with all people, including children.

In May 1984, he befriended Juanita White, a single mother of two children, 14-year old Vernita White, and her younger brother. After befriending Juanita over a few weeks, he then asked for permission from Juanita to have Vernita accompany him to his house to pick up a stereo system on May 29th. Both never came back, and Vernita was found brutally murdered, raped, and bound with a TV cord.

Then, in the company of Debra, his girlfriend, they abducted two children, Tamika, and Annie as they walked and left school for home. The two were very young, seven and nine, respectively. The two depraved beings then tied up the children, and when Tamika couldn't stop crying, Debra covered her mouth while Coleman, without remorse, stepped on her chest. But they were not done. They killed her by strangulation, then both defiled Annie beat her and choked her, but Annie lived through the ordeal.

Then, on the same day, they abducted Donna Williams, from Indiana, who had known Coleman for a few weeks. She was found on July 11th, 1984. She had been strangled, and her car was close by. What this even scarier was that the incident took place just a short distance from Coleman's grandma's house.

Then, they were in Ohio four days passed, where they gained the trust of another African American family, headed by Virginia Temple. Temple had three children, with Rachelle, 9, being the oldest. The pair strangled Virginia and Rachelle and then put their bodies in the crawlspace in the home's basement. The other two children were not harmed, and Virginia's mother found them when she came to visit.

Theirs was also merely a murder seemingly for the thrill of it, an indictment into the twist of human psychology when you dig deep.

According to Del Paulhus, a personality psychologist, the four dark personalities - Machiavellian, Narcissism, Psychopathy and Sadism, these personalities are fascinating than the typical personality types, which could explain our obsession with serial killers and their actions of extreme, often without any apparent motive.

Del Paulhus called for more linking between these dark personalities typed, despite their distinct concepts.

Looking at it, you get the sense that, indeed, they are part of the same basic structure. All four personality types often will be reflective of the doers' view of the world. To kill, you will need a set of distinguishing traits, after all, to begin to murder, then keep murdering, and with increasing violence and seeming glee.

On their own, these cases of call for us to give more attention to what precisely the dark psychology is and how we can look into it further. Beneath our human conscience, lies a dark underworld, waiting for just the right trigger to come to the fore.

Conclusion

Thank for making it through to the end of Dark Psychology Secrets, let's hope it was informative and able to provide you with all of the tools you need to achieve your goals whatever they may be.

The following step is to start learning and using some of the techniques found in this guidebook. There are times when all of us want to be able to manipulate and influence those around us. We want to get others to help us finish a project, we want them to agree with us on something and side with us, or we even want someone to purchase a product from us. And all of these things are going to require us to learn how to use the power of persuasion and manipulation to get it done.

This guidebook took some time to explore this power, and how we cannot only use it to help us get further in life but also to recognize when someone else is using it against us. Being able to take care of ourselves, so others are not able to attack us and use mind control, and more on us can make a big difference in the life we live, and how much control we have over our thoughts and decisions. This guidebook is going to help us learn how to make this happen rightly.

From here, the sky is your limit—you are free to do as you choose. You can choose to delve into more of the vastly fascinating world of dark psychology, or you can attempt to utilize the skills provided in this book. Remember, this book was just a peek into this world—there are several more techniques to dark subliminal psychology, and there are several more areas of dark psychology that may interest you. No matter where you find yourself headed, however, you should remember that the skills you learned in here can be dangerous. Subliminal psychology is not a toy and should be treated with the respect and care it deserves. If you are unwilling to do so, you are far more likely to cause more harm than good as you attempt to navigate through the world wielding these skills.

When you are ready to learn more about manipulation, and how to get the most out of manipulation and dark psychology possible. When you are ready to learn more about these techniques, and all of the different methods and tools that you can use with it, make sure to check out this guidebook and learn how to make these work for you.

Good luck on your journey, and feel free to come back to re-read this guidebook from time to time if you need a refresher or some more information on subliminal psychology.

Manipulation

Introduction

Manipulation is using people's emotions and behavioral traits deliberately to obtain what is desired. Manipulators use their ability to understand others and get what they want by using trickery, misdirection, persuasion, charm, and coaxing.

In the mind of a manipulator, he or she thinks, "I have the ability to change people's behavior and let them give me what I want." Skilled manipulators can even come out of a situation when they get caught trying to use other people to their advantage.

A manipulator has a tendency to create a certain level of strain in a situation. They use multiple techniques to mold their personality according to their goals. A manipulator can make you feel on top of the world, or the worst person on this planet. It all depends on how that manipulator wants you to act.

Manipulation, as a concept, involves two parties. One is the manipulator and the other is manipulated. While manipulators are extremely aware of their surroundings, some personalities tend to ignore that. People, who are emotionally vulnerable or don't have a clear mindset, tend to get manipulated.

Generally speaking, everyone manipulates without knowing. Lying or hiding the complete story are a few common ways of manipulation; however, manipulators live these tactics as the way of their lives. They use various tactics as their tools to fool you into doing what they want.

That's why you need to understand all types of manipulation and more importantly, learn how to address it positively in different aspects of your life.

Different Types of Manipulation

If you aren't aware enough, manipulators can use many techniques to control you. They change their approach depending on the victim's personality, so they first observe you and learn your core personality traits. At the core, you can be a loving person, a lonely person, naïve or too confident.

With personality observation, manipulators create their tactic to attack you. Here are different types of manipulation that you need to become aware of:

1. Hiding the complete story

You can notice this in your office, parties and other conversations taking place around you. There are people who hide certain portions of stories in order to create a diversion. The listener of the story gets to know what the manipulator wants him to know.

What if a colleague in your office tells you how others are bitching about you! It is possible that you are getting half of the side of the story, but if you are unaware of manipulation, this half story can trigger emotions like anger and hatred, and you end up doing something that you regret.

When a manipulator uses a half story, they don't lie. They just avoid telling certain portions so that you see a picture of their creation. The tactic behind this method is to stay on the safe side. If exposed, the manipulator can simply say that he or she has explained nothing but the truth and in doing so, you risk facing humiliation due to your wrong actions.

2. Lying

Generally, people lie when they are scared or want to get out of an unwanted situation, but a manipulator's lie is different. Their lies always have a purpose or an end goal. In fact, they don't even have to plan before lying. They can plan their next lie while having a conversation with you.

Depending on what they want, manipulators can choose different lies to make you their victim. It is a blend of thrill and excitement they feel while trying to play your personality.

3. Love and charm

Narcissistic manipulators use love and charm to control you. This behavior is majorly visible in love relationships between partners. You get hooked and think that your partner loves you the most. They charm and create an illusion of a perfect relationship. These people always want something from you.

When love has built the foundation, the manipulator uses that to control you. They can ask for things, money or just play with your emotions. The goals depend on the personality of the manipulator. Some people have the disorder to love and then hurt their partners. The roots of this behavior lead back to their own previous experiences.

To spot the manipulation of love, you need to notice who is making decisions in your relationship:

- Do you feel afraid of your partner when making a personal choice?

- Has it become your habit to get your partner's approval on everything?

- Are you doing things that you wouldn't do otherwise?

These questions can help you decipher love manipulation in your daily life.

4. Changing behavior frequently

This is different than changing personality traits according to a victim. A manipulator, many times, may showcase a behavioral change towards the same person again and again. Now, you can think of all those people who seem different every time you meet them. This behavior is common in love relationships, and boss and employee relationships as well.

The manipulator wants you to stay malleable and out of balance so, one minute he or she can look happy, and swiftly become angry for no valid reason. However, they make you think that their behavioral switch has a legitimate reason. Your boss can start shouting angrily just for a single typo in your report. Similarly, a manipulative partner can come home with a different mood every day.

We, as humans, understand other people's personalities before socializing. You feel more comfortable around a person who you know well, instead of a stranger, but manipulators use their mood swings to keep you scared and afraid of them. You feel unaware of their personalities and try to please them.

5. Denying accusations

A manipulator can deny things very impressively. If you accuse them of something, they confidently present a believable story. The confidence, combined with an impressive story, makes you believe them.

Denying accusations is the simplest form of manipulation. In fact, this is the first tactic that manipulators use in their early ages. A kid with manipulative tendencies usually denies things with confidence and makes stories to justify their case.

6. Punishments

Punishment is a disciplinary action to control other people's behavior. This is also a manipulation technique that gives your control to a manipulator. Physical violence, shouting, and nagging are the visible techniques of manipulation.

Apart from that, you can also get emotionally punished with the silence of a person or mental abuse. A manipulator can attack your emotional vulnerabilities to make you feel bad. They keep on doing it until you start behaving exactly the way they want. Such manipulation is seen in marriages a lot. One partner uses physical and mental abuse to control the other. Also, you can notice these manipulation symptoms in a parent-kid relationship. A manipulative kid can use the silent treatment to control his or her mother.

7. Blaming for overreaction

Is there a person who makes you feel bad about yourself?! That person can be a manipulator.

Using the blame game allows a manipulator to put you on the faulty side of every conversation. If you point out their actions, they blame you for overreacting. They say that you are reacting way too much for a very small thing. This way they become the victim and you end up feeling bad about your own actions.

8. Victim targeting

You are the victim, but the accuser makes you defend yourself in front of others. This way, the manipulator masks his or her own wrongdoings by shifting the focus towards you. The manipulator does it all in front of you, but you feel out of control of the situation.

9. Playing a victim

Have you ever helped people whom you never liked as a person? Then it is possible that you were used with this manipulation technique.

Manipulators play victim from time to time to gain compassion and sympathy. Their end goal is always to use you in some way; however, not every victim is a manipulator. Some are genuinely hurt and require your support, but manipulators can use your helping nature to get what they want.

10. Too much positive attention

The corporate world is filled with such manipulators nowadays. People use expensive presents, give money, and praise to lure you towards them. Excessive charm and too much attention are used for people who seek approval and like getting praised. Manipulators judge personalities and give too much attention to satisfy your emotional needs.

Positive attention works if you are emotionally vulnerable. For instance, if you mention "society" before taking every action, it tells a manipulator about your approval-seeking nature. Your high-class dressing sense and money-focused behavior also give signals to manipulators. They start giving you the royal treatment and manipulate in the process.

11. Diversions

Shifting situations and conversations are also manipulation techniques. You feel you know what's going on, but suddenly a person changes the whole picture. If that happens in your life frequently, then there is a manipulator around you. He or she wants you to stay confused, while they get to twist situations in their favor.

When in a group conversation, a manipulator plays the role of a narrator. If a conversation goes against his or her plan, they immediately shift the topic to something else. These manipulators become the kings and queens of office politics.

12. Isolation

Manipulation is difficult when you are consulting your family and friends on the same topic; hence, a manipulator tries everything to isolate you from other people. This doesn't have to be a literal isolation. The manipulator can tell you to keep things a secret from everyone. Once you agree to that, he or she can twist your behavior easily.

Covert and Overt Types of Manipulation

Covert and overt are two major categories of manipulation.

Covert manipulation combines all the invisible techniques of manipulation. You can't see the psychological attacks of an abuser until it's done. This type of manipulation is intentional, and the abuser prepares to harm you in a psychological way.

You think that all the wrong things are happening accidentally, but the abuser knows what you feel. The extreme covert manipulators are known as psychopaths and narcissists. They follow a systematic emotional attack to break your confidence and control your realities, and you end up as their puppet without knowing that at all.

In covert manipulation, the abuser shows you a twisted reality. This misguided reality brainwashes you and ruins your ability to make correct decisions; then, the abuser guides as he or she pleases.

Overt manipulation includes all those techniques, which the victim can experience and notice, so the physical, verbal and sexual abuses come into this category. It is a situation where you have a higher tendency of knowing that you are being manipulated, but some folks may still end up not knowing what to do about it.

Both overt and covert manipulation deserve to be on your watch list that is for sure, and we will find ways to deal with them later on!

The Different Types of Manipulators

According to the manipulation techniques, you can come across the following kinds of manipulators:

The Expert

"I am better than you at everything."

This person wants to stay on top of every situation. These manipulators are driven by their desire to attain a strong social dominance over others. Their personalities include a high ego, which they blend with their ability to locate vulnerable people. These people like to keep people who lack self-confidence, which serves their ego.

Using insults and put-downs, these manipulators exploit the vulnerability of their victims. They are narcissistic but hide their arrogance with fake politeness. At the core, these manipulators have self-doubts and shame. Manipulation becomes their technique to hide their own vulnerability.

The Perpetual Victim

"People hurt me and use me all the time."

In every scenario, you find these manipulators showcasing themselves as victims. Even if the situation has nothing to do with them, they find a way to become the victim. If you cut your fingers by mistake, this manipulator starts getting a headache and blames you for that.

By becoming a victim, these manipulators cause fights and arguments around them. You might argue with others for this person, and they stay behind the scenes and, after every argument or fight, this person will behave as a victim again. This gives power to emotionally control others and gain their sympathy at the same time.

These manipulators seek more attention from their surroundings. You can see them feeling angry and emotionally distressed. They blame their shortcomings on others' hatred for them. They use "ethics" as their manipulation card so many times and project paranoia about everything.

Strong Dependents

"Please follow my lead to save me from my life."

These manipulators are strong and weak at the same time. They present themselves as a powerless creature, but they are very much in control from the inside. They like to depend on someone else for their needs. In order to gain that control, they show as if they are weak and unable to live on their own. Giving compliments is the secret weapon they use to obtain control over victims.

The moment you judge them as inferior and try to help, they gain control over you. One by one, all their responsibilities become yours, and if you try to avoid them, they make you feel as if you are letting them down like how others have.

The Angry Beast

"How dare you ask me that, it is not my fault at all!"

These manipulators won't let you blame them for anything. They keep people away by using anger as their guard. Teenagers usually showcase these tendencies for a while; however, they aren't aware of their behavior. On the other hand, a manipulator deliberately shows anger.

In many relationships, one partner shows anger if asked about stealing behavior, increasing credit card bills, or cheating. No matter how politely you ask, their reply is always over the top. They constantly avoid confrontation and play the blame game with their partner. For example, a manipulator can blame the partner for his/her affair saying, "I had an affair because you weren't spending enough time with me." A strong denial is their key to keep doing what they want to do so they can scream or physically abuse you if confronted strongly.

The Wrong Well-wisher

"I am the only friend you have in this world. Others want to eat you alive."

Lying, hiding the complete story and other manipulation techniques are valuable tools for these manipulators. They want to isolate you from family and friends by feeding lies in your mind. At the same time, they present themselves as your only well-wisher who is on your side no matter what. Alliance creation is the way they live their lives. Their friendly nature doesn't allow you to figure out their true intentions. They gradually create a strong bond with their victim, keeping their nasty intentions hidden. Then, the series of rumors begin, and the manipulator becomes the source of information for the victim. They hurt emotionally with their lies and trigger hatred and anger in their victim's mind.

Friends, parents or colleagues, anyone can be this manipulator in your life. For instance, between two close girlfriends, one can start spreading rumors about another's character, just because she has a crush on her friend's boyfriend.

The Truth Twister

"Sorry, I think I have misinterpreted what you told me."

Using half-truths, exaggerations, and lies, these manipulators gain control over victims. They smartly alter the victim's words and turn them into reputation-harming rumors. When exposed, they simply deny and apologize by saying, "I misunderstood your words." These people want to feel superior in their group, even if they don't deserve it. Their friendly nature allows them to blend and bond with people to exploit their vulnerable sides. Gaining personal information is the first step they make, and then they create a misinterpreted story around that information. They have the capacity to justify their actions and play victim if confronted.

The Stubborn Deniers

"You are bad, and I am good. Period."

Filled with a vast amount of ego, these manipulators deny their own behavior and actions. They usually don't understand their own flaws and project those flaws in others. For example, such a manipulator can say, "You are a racist person," even when they have racist tendencies. They see their faults and think that the world has those faults. These manipulators blame their victims and even try to include other people in their blame game. Their stubborn nature doesn't let them realize their own flaws. They actually believe that their actions and beliefs are always right.

For example, such a manipulator will point out the laziness of their victim, when he is the lazy one. In his mind, he will create justifications for his own laziness.

The Charming Flirt

"I am gorgeous, so give me what I want."

Attracting people and controlling them, that is how these manipulators operate. Their attractive looks become their weapon. Superficial in nature, these people feel more attractive than they actually are. They have to be the favorite person in every person's life; however, they only care about their needs and desires. Flirtatious nature and sexual triggers help these manipulators lure their victims. They want you to react to their flirtatious behavior in a positive way. These manipulators love creating tension among family members and friends.

These manipulators never stop looking for new partners. They connect with current partners strongly but keep looking for new potential partners. They don't believe in traditional relationship structures of society. In fact, when friendships and families break, it empowers these manipulators. They want to twist people's relationships and live life like a grand drama show.

Chapter 11.Powerful Techniques to Manipulate, Persuade and Influence Anyone

Persuasion Techniques

There are many ways to persuade people to think or behave in your favor. The following strategies are all methods of persuasion that you will want to master. Ideally, you will work on one or two at a time. If you try and rush it all, it may become extremely obvious as to what you are trying to do, and people may see through it. The goal is to practice something until you can seamlessly integrate it with your regular conversation so that no one even recognizes you are doing so. Over time, you can add in more and more, until you have completely mastered the art of persuasion.

Pacing

This ultimately means that you mirror someone else's behavior and language. When you can do so, you create a subconscious sense of connection between you and the individual you are talking to. You don't want to be extremely obvious when doing this, so don't entirely mirror them, but you want to do it enough that you create that subconscious message. If they touch their hair, you could fix yours. If you see that they are leaning to the left, wait a few moments and then naturally lean over to the left as well. When they say certain things, find a way to naturally work those words into the conversations so that they feel like you "get" them. This will help them feel connected to you and will assist them in establishing a sense of trust with you. When someone trusts you, they are much more likely to do what it is that you desire for them to do.

Pacing is the very first step of getting control in a conversation. When you pace, you give yourself the ability to subliminally tap into their subconscious and put them into a hypnotic state. They have no idea that you are doing so, so this is why it is considered such a powerful form of mind control. You will use this as your foundation to begin your brainwashing techniques.

Embedding

Once you have established the pacing part of the conversation, you can begin practicing embedding. This is the process whereby you embed certain commands into your conversations so that they begin to think in your favor. You are not directly telling them to do so, but because you are speaking into their subconscious mind you do hold an authority position where in suggesting it, you make them naturally want to do so.

Embedding commands into the conversation may seem difficult, but it is actually rather easy, and it will have your listener deciding in your favor without you ever having to convince them to do so. You always want to make sure that you are embedding commands seamlessly so that they sound natural, and so that they don't sound like a command at all. You will learn about some real-life scenarios, but one example you can consider right now would be if you were to want someone to take you on a date. Say you are having a conversation with them, you could say something such as "So, do you go on dates often?" by naturally working up to this phrase and then injecting it into the conversation, you give the listener the idea that they want to take you on a date. Then, they will make the decision without you ever having to outright ask or command it, or even have to make it seem like it was your idea to begin with.

Primary Motivators

Primary motivators are ultimately the reasons why someone would want to do what you are asking of them. There are many motivators, and you want to be certain that you structure them in the right way so that they motivate your listener and get the momentum building. By structuring your weaker and more powerful points properly, you can create an irreversible momentum that will get anyone working in your favor.

The best way to do this is to identify your primary motivators, and then identify your minor motivators. You want to use your primary motivators as the first and last part of motivation in your conversation, and then you want to inject the minor ones throughout the rest of the conversation. That way, the person you are talking to knows what the purpose of the conversation is from the beginning and leaves the conversation with the purpose in mind as well. The fillers in the middle will all just provide extra information as to why they should make their decision in your favor.

Repetition

There is a very high value that comes along with repetition. That is why advertisements are repeated everywhere, and why you can see them on many different platforms. That is why businesspeople will give you a call back and do their best to regularly put their company name in front of your eyes. That is why when you hear about something several times, you are more interested in it and more likely to engage with it than you are if you only hear about it once. This is the same for your listener.

When you are having a conversation, repeat the same thing in various ways. Find new ways to present the information in a way that doesn't make you sound like a broken record but helps your listener to stay focused on something. This idea is that they warm up to your information more and more each time, and eventually they are ready to decide in your favor.

You want to make sure that you make the repetition natural, and that you span it out over multiple conversations or interactions if necessary. This will ensure that this particular persuasion technique works, and that the outcome is in your favor.

Anchoring

Anchoring is a very popular form of persuasion or mind control that uses physical action to talk to the subconscious mind. Anchoring is extremely easy in theory but takes some practice in order to be able to do it in a way that actually works.

Essentially, anchoring works by "anchoring" one part of your body to "good" information, and one part to "bad" information. So, let's say you want to convince someone to travel to Spain instead of France. Anytime you talk about Spain you will naturally touch or point to one area on your body, let's say your left shoulder. However, anytime you talk about France you will touch or point to another area on your body, let's say the right hip. You want to make it very unobvious that you are doing this, so you don't want to clearly be pointing directly to this spot. Ideally, you will just casually gesture towards them and sometimes touch them. As a result, your listener will associate each area on your body with a certain point. They will see your left shoulder as "good" and your right hip as "bad". So, when you finally get to the punchline, if you say "So, where would you like to go?" while you are gesturing towards your left shoulder. As a result, their subconscious mind will be more likely to get their conscious mind to say Spain, because they have naturally associated your left shoulder with Spain which is "good".

Manipulation Techniques

Being able to manipulate someone's thoughts is actually not as difficult as you may suspect, and it can have a powerful effect on your ability to get them to think in the way that you want them to think so that you can have your desired outcome.

There are seven ways that people can manipulate others. Unlike persuasion, these are not techniques that you use necessarily in conversation, such as anchoring or pacing. Rather, these are other important techniques that are involved in the relationship you build with the people you are talking to, and how you can use that relationship to manipulate them to have certain thoughts and decisions that work in your favor. The following strategies are an important part of manipulation.

Trust

Having the trust of the people you are talking to is important. When people trust you, they are much more likely to actually listen to you. They will feel more compelled to have conversations with you, they will be more likely to respect what you say, and they will be more likely to agree with you or comply with you when you exercise authority.

Gaining trust in your relationship comes from using tactics such as mirroring, as well as by generally being trustworthy. Show that you genuinely care about what they are saying, and that you have an interest in their wellbeing. Make them feel as though they can feel confident in your ability to think for their better interest so that they don't have to when they are with you. This way, when you make a request, suggestion, or subliminal command, they are much more likely to comply because they know you think with their best interest at heart.

Cause

You have to have cause when you are using any type of manipulation strategy. This means that you have a good reason why someone should do something. When you have a cause or reason why they would want to or should want to do anything, they are much more likely to actually want to do it. The incredible thing about manipulation and mindset is that you don't actually need to have an extremely great cause. As long as the cause is something that can be perceived as important and relevant, you can use it and it will work!

Secret Hypnosis

Secretly hypnotizing people without them knowing it is a powerful form of manipulation. Technically, you achieve this by using persuasion techniques such as pacing and anchoring. The reason why we mention this under the manipulation position is because it is important and relevant in both strategies. If you want to be able to successfully persuade and manipulate people to do what you want them to do, you need to be able to secretly hypnotize them. This is also relevant and important for deception and particularly subliminal messages.

When you have people under secret hypnosis, you can speak directly to their subconscious and you don't have to worry about their conscious mind getting in the way. While you do still need to accommodate for their conscious mind in the conversation, you have a direct passage to their subconscious mind to help activate your mind control strategies. It is important to understand how important this process is and activate it in every conversation when you want to be in control.

Using Their Feelings

Arguing with logic can be hard because most people are driven by feelings, not logic. Even if they are highly logical people, they are more likely to be driven by logic and emotions, not merely logic. That is why getting into their emotional state and using their feelings to get desired results is often the best way to get what you want.

Proof of Results

People have always been more likely to act when there is proof that the results are what they are looking for. This is why having proof of the results they can expect when doing what you say will be extremely helpful in getting your way. Think about it this way: humans are herd animals; we do not like to be left behind or feel as though we are the odd one out. If you have proof that others have done it, then the people you are talking to are going to want to be one of those people, too. They will not want to be left out or feel as though they are the only ones not doing it, so they will naturally feel infinitely more inclined because they want to follow the herd.

Authority

People are naturally more inclined to comply to someone who speaks and acts with authority, instead of someone who appears to be intimidated or uncertain about what they are saying. If you are uncertain, waiver in your stance, or otherwise appear to be under confident, people are going to pick up on this and will feel less compelled to listen to you. They do not like to follow those who are not confident and strong. This could potentially lead them into a situation they don't want to be in. However, if you are leading with authority through confidence, strength, and certainty, people are going to assume that you know what you are talking about and they will feel more inclined to listen and comply.

Manipulation works heavily through knowing how to assert yourself in a conversation and use a human's nature against them. By understanding how people naturally behave, act, and think, you can use this to your advantage and create a situation that will allow you to carry the control in the conversation and manipulate people's thoughts and feelings to work in your favor.

Deception Techniques

Deception, as you know, is the process where you deceive someone instead of lying to them. In other words, you are knowingly omitting the truth and preventing someone from finding out through the way you guide the conversation. Deception in and of itself is a technique, though there are certain key points you can remember as an opportunity to maximize your deceptive abilities and have success with deception in conversation.

Avoid the Topic

The first and ultimately easiest way to exercise deception is to avoid the topic altogether. For example, if you do not want your boss to know that you weren't actually sick when you skipped work the other day, you would simply want to avoid the topic altogether. Without it ever coming up, you are never put into a situation where you have to actually use deception. This is a form of deception itself because you are allowing your boss to believe that you were truly sick, and you are omitting the truth from them. This is easy because you never have to actually use any of the other techniques with deception. You can simply rely on skirting the topic to allow your boss to continue believing that you were away sick, when in reality you were not sick at all but simply wanted or needed the day off for an alternative purpose.

Do Not Lie

Deception is different from lying in that you are not saying anything that isn't true. You are not telling something that is false, and therefore you are not lying. Instead, you are leading someone to believe false information through careful intention when you guide conversations. If you want to successfully deceive someone, you must refrain from lying at all costs. Lying puts the blame on you: the person can question why you were not truthful when you were asked something outright. However, when you deceive someone, the blame is on them. They were the ones who chose to believe without requiring further information, therefore they are the ones who are responsible for not having found out additional information. You can easily say "You never asked" when they ask why you never told them. This puts it on them, and away from you. They cannot blame you or generate a sense of mistrust based on the fact that you told an outright lie to them.

Careful Wording

Your wording is how you can avoid lying and instead use deception in conversation. You want to make sure that you carefully word things to lead someone to believe what you want them to believe, without actually lying to them to get them to believe it. For example, when you were calling for that sick day, you may have simply called in and said, "I need to take a sick day today." Nothing more, nothing less. Since you took a sick day, your boss will likely assume that you were actually sick. However, you never admitted to being sick, rather you simply stated that you needed to take a sick day. In other words, you were using your sick day as an opportunity to get the time off that you needed on that day.

The same goes for anything. You want to make sure that you are carefully wording your sentence to lead someone in one direction, without actually lying to get them there. Take your time, practice your wording, and look for loopholes that you can use to get people to believe you. This is how you can master deception.

Deceptive Actions

Deception can go much further than conversation and wording, as well. Deceptive actions can also assist you in achieving your desired result. This means that you act based on the truth you want them to believe, and not the realistic truth. For example, let's say you like your friend's spouse. Since you don't want them to find out, you can avoid the conversation and act as though you are merely friends with their spouse. You do not show that you are interested in them, you simply feel it and continue acting as regular friends with that person. You treat them the same as you would treat any other friend. This is deception through activity. You are not leading anyone to the truth, even though it exists. Instead, you are leading them in the other direction. You have never admitting to liking or not liking their spouse, it is simply assumed that you don't, and your actions help lead people towards believing the same thing.

Chapter 12.NLP Manipulation Techniques

What is Neuro Linguistic Programming?

Neuro Linguistic Programming, or NLP, in simplest terms is the programming language of your mind. We've all had instances where we attempted to communicate with someone who doesn't speak our language. The outcome? They didn't understand us!

You go to a restaurant abroad and ask for a fancy steak but end up receiving insipid stew owing to the misinterpretation of language and codes.

This is precisely what happens when we try to communicate with our subconscious mind. We think we are commanding it to give us happier relationships, more money, a better job and other, similar things. However, if that's not what is actually showing up, something is being lost in translation. The subconscious/unconscious mind has the power to help us accomplish our goals only if we program it using codes it recognizes and understands.

If you are asking your unconscious mind for steak and receiving stew, it is time to speak its language. Think of NLP as a user manual for the brain. When people master NLP, they become fluent in the language of the subconscious mind, which is excellent when it comes to re-programming their own and other people's thoughts, ideas and beliefs. This gives them the power to influence and persuade people, and on the downside, even manipulate them.

Neuro Linguistic Programming is a set of techniques, methods and tools for enhancing communication with deeper layers of our brain. It is an approach that combines personal development, psychotherapy and communication. Its creators (John Grinder and Richard Bandler) claim that there is a strong link between language, behavior patterns and neurological processes, which can be used for enhancing learning and personal development.

Influence versus Manipulation

So, do you believe a hammer is a tool of utility or destruction? Well, it depends on how you use it, right? Or what purpose you use it for.

NLP is potent when it comes to getting people to do what you want them to. It is the hammer that can be used to fix a nail in the wall or destroy a piece of wood. Similarly, NLP can be used to build something positive, or it can be used for a destructive purpose (manipulation).

NLP and manipulation have nearly the same meaning. Both are about generating the desired effect on other people without obvious exertion. However, one key difference between influence and manipulation is that the latter is meant to influence others to meet the manipulator's selfish goals through means that can be unfair, unlawful, sneaky, or insidious. Things are contrived through underhanded methods to turn out in favor of the manipulator. A manipulator often preys on the insecurities, fears and guilt of other people. In turn, victims of manipulation feed dissatisfied, frustrated, trapped and unhappy.

Conversely, influence is the ability to inspire people in an admirable, charismatic and honorable way. We are often inspired by influential people and aspire to model our life on theirs. There is a general feeling of positivity related to them, and we feel positively impacted in their company. Not every influence is positive, which is why we use terms such as "bad influence" to signify a person's negative effect on us. However, manipulation is never categorized as good or bad. It always operates with sinister motives. That is the primary difference between influence and manipulation.

Influence is a double-edged sword that can be used positively and negatively, while manipulation only operates with a negative, narrow and selfish perspective to meet the objectives of the manipulator.

While manipulation has self-centered and questionable motives, influence can also be positive. In contrast to manipulation, influence has positive connotations, which considers other people's needs, goals and desires. Don't we, as parents, want to influence our children to lead happier and healthier lives? Similarly, as a manager, we want to influence our team to put in their best efforts.

How is NLP Used for Manipulating People?

NLP training is conducted in a pyramid-like structure, with sophisticated techniques reserved for high-end seminars. It is a complex subject (whoever said anything related to the human mind would be easy?). However, to simplify a complicated concept, NLPers, or people who practice NLP, pay keen attention to people they work with. They watch everything from eye movements to skin flushes to pupil dilation in order to determine what type of information people are processing.

Through observation, NLPers can tell which side of the brain is dominant in a person. Similarly, they can tell what sense is the most active within the person's brain. The eye movements can determine how their brain stores and uses information. It is also easy to decipher whether the person is stating facts (telling the truth) or making up facts (lying) by looking at his/her eye movements.

After gathering this invaluable information, NLP manipulators will subtly mirror and mimic their victims (including speech, body language, mannerisms, verbal linguistic patterns and more) to give a feeling of being 'one among them.'

NLPers will fake social clues to lead their victims into dropping their guard and entering a more open, receptive and suggestible state of mind, where they become ready to absorb whatever information their mind is fed. Manipulators will cleverly use language that focuses on a person's predominant senses.

For example, if a person is focused on his/her visual sense, the NLP manipulator will most likely use it to his/her advantage optimally by saying something like, "Do you see where I am coming from?" "Can you see what I am trying to tell you?" or "See it this way?" Similarly, if a person is a predominantly auditory person, the manipulator will speak to them using auditory metaphors like, "Just hear me out once, Tim" or "I hear you."

By mirroring their victim's body language and verbal linguistic patterns, NLP experts, or NLPer manipulators, attempt to accomplish a clear objective – building rapport. Manipulators also try to accomplish this by sharing too much too soon or building early intimacy. The objective is the same – to strike a rapport with their victims, which then makes it easy for the victims to let down their guard.

Once the manipulator uses NLP to build rapport and get the victim to let down his guard through clever use of body language and verbal patterns, the victim becomes more open and suggestible. Fake social cues are fed to the victim to make their minds more malleable.

Once they build a rapport, NLPers will begin to lead the victim into increased interaction in a sublime manner. After having mirrored the victim and establishing in the victim's subconscious mind that he/she (the manipulator) is one among them (the victim), the manipulator increases his/her chances of getting the victim to do whatever the manipulator wants. They will subtly change their behavior and language to influence their victim's actions.

The techniques can include leading questions, sublime language patterns and a host of other NLP techniques to maneuver the person's mind wherever they want. The victim, on the other hand, often doesn't realize what is happening. In their view, everything is occurring naturally/organically or according to their consent.

Of course, manipulators (however skilled) may not be able to use NLP to get people to behave in a manner that is completely out of character. However, it can be used to steer people's responses in the desired direction. For instance, you can't convince a fundamentally ethical and truthful person to act in a dishonest manner. However, you can use it to get a person to think in a specific direction or line of thought. Manipulators use NLP to engineer specific responses from a person.

NLP attempts accomplish two ends, eliciting and anchoring. Eliciting occurs when NLPers use language and leading to draw their victims into an emotional state. Once the desired state is accomplished, the NLPer will then anchor the emotion with a specific physical clue - for example, tapping on their shoulder. This simply means that an NLPer can invoke the same emotion in you by tapping your shoulder.

For example, let us say the NLP manipulator makes you feel depressed or unworthy using language, leading and other NLP techniques. This is followed by tapping the back of your hands in a specific manner to create anchoring. Thus, each time they want to create an emotion of being disillusioned, depressed and unworthy in you, they will tap the back of your palm. It is nothing but conditioning you to feel in a certain way with linked physical clues.

Now that you have a fair idea of what NLP is or how manipulators can use it for submission, what can you do to guard yourself against NLP manipulators?

Here are some tips to prevent NLPers from pulling their remarkably smart yet sneaky tricks on you:

1. Be wary of people mirroring your body language. Agreed, you didn't know this until now, but people imitating or copying your body language

is one of the biggest red flags of them trying to manipulate, influence or persuade you to act in a desired manner. I really enjoy testing these NLP experts using subtle hand gestures and leg movements to gauge if they are indeed mirroring my body language to establish a rapport.

If they follow suit, that's my clue to flee! Experienced NLPers have mastered the art of subtle mirroring, which means you may not even realize they are imitating your actions. NLP beginners will instantly imitate the exact same movement in their eagerness to establish a feeling of oneness. Good way for you to call their bluff!

2. Confuse with eye movements. Another fantastic way to call an NLP manipulator's bluff is to notice if they are paying very close attention to your eyes or eye movements. NLP users often examine their target or victim's very carefully. The eye movements are scrutinized to gauge how you access and store information.

In effect, they want to determine what parts of the brain you are utilizing to gather clues about your thoughts and feelings. I say beat this by darting your eyes all around the place randomly. Move them upwards and downwards or from side to side in no clear pattern. You are throwing your NLP manipulator off course. Make it appear natural. Their calibration will go down the wayside.

3. Beware of people's touch. One of the techniques NLPers use is anchoring. If you know a person practices NLP, and you are in an especially heightened or intense emotional condition, do not allow them to touch you in any manner. Just throw them off course by suddenly laughing hard or flying into a fit of rage. Basically, you are confusing them

about the emotion they need to anchor. Even if they attempt to establish a physical clue to invoke certain emotions, they'll be left with a mixed bag of crazy laughter, rage and whatever else you did.

4. Watch out for permissive language. Typical language used by NLPers includes "be relaxed," "relax and enjoy this," and other similar statements. Beware of this NLP, hypnotist style language that induces you into a state of deep relaxation or trance to get you to think or act in a specific manner. Skilled or covert manipulators rarely command in a straightforward manner.

They will cleverly seek your permission to give you the impression that you are doing what they want you to do out of your own free will (one of their many sinister tricks). If you observe experienced hypnotists, they will never outright command you to do anything but seek your permission to make it appear as if it is being done organically, with your consent.

5. Guard Against Gibberish. Watch out for mumbo jumbo that just doesn't make any logical sense or twisted/complicated statements that mean little. For example, "As you free the feeling of being held by your thoughts, you will find yourself in alignment with the voice of your success." Does this make any sense? NLP manipulators won't say anything purposeful, but rather, they will program your emotional state to lead it where they want to.

One of the best ways to guard against this sort of hypnotism-NLP induced manipulation is to urge the manipulator to be more specific. "Can you be clearer about this?" "Can you specify exactly what you mean by that?" It won't just interrupt their cleverly set technique but will also force the interaction into precise language, thus breaking the trance brought about through ambiguous words and phrases.

6. Don't quickly agree to anything. If you find yourself being compelled to make an instant decision about something important, and it feels like you are steered in a specific direction, escape the situation. Wait a day to make a decision. Do not be swept or led into making a decision that you do not want to make on an impulse. Sales professionals are adept at manipulating buyers into purchasing something they don't need using sneaky manipulation and NLP tactics. When someone rushes you into a decision, it should be a warning signal to back off and hold on until you've thought more about the situation.

Chapter 13. How Toxic People Chose their Favorite Victims

There are certain characteristics and behavioral traits that make people more vulnerable to manipulation, and people with dark psychology traits know this full well. They tend to seek out victims who have those specific behavioral traits because they are essentially easy targets. Let's discuss 6 of the traits of the favorite victims of manipulators.

Emotional insecurity and fragility

Manipulators like to target victims who are emotionally insecure or emotionally fragile. Unfortunately for these victims, such traits are very easy to identify even in total strangers, so it's easy for experienced manipulators to find them.

People who are emotionally insecure tend to be very defensive when they are attacked or when they are under pressure, and that makes them easy to spot in social situations. Even after just a few interactions, a manipulator can gauge with a certain degree of accuracy, how insecure a person is. They'll try to provoke their potential targets in a subtle way, and then wait to see how the targets react. If they are overly defensive, manipulators will take it as a sign of insecurity, and they will intensify their manipulative attacks.

Manipulators can also tell if a target is emotionally insecure if he/she redirects accusations or negative comments. They will find a way to put you on the spot, and if you try to throw it back at them, or to make excuses instead of confronting the situation head-on, the manipulator could conclude that you are insecure and therefore an easy target.

People who have social anxiety also tend to have emotional insecurity, and manipulators are aware of this fact. In social gatherings, they can easily spot individuals who have social anxiety, then target them for manipulation. "Pickup artists" are able to identify the girls who seem uneasy in social situations by the way they conduct themselves. Social anxiety is difficult to conceal, especially to manipulators who are experienced at preying on emotional vulnerability.

Emotional fragility is different from emotional insecurity. Emotionally insecure people tend to show it all the time, while emotionally fragile people appear to be normal, but they break down emotionally at the slightest provocation. Manipulators like targeting emotionally fragile people because it's very easy to elicit a reaction from them. Once a manipulator finds out that you are emotionally fragile, he is going to jump at the change to manipulate you because he knows it would be fairly easy.

Emotional fragility can be temporary, so people with these traits are often targeted by opportunistic manipulators. A person may be emotionally stable most of the time, but he/she may experience emotional fragility when they are going through a breakup, when they are grieving, or when they are dealing with a situation that is emotionally draining. The more diabolical manipulators can earn your trust, bid their time, and wait for you to be emotionally fragile. Alternatively, they can use underhanded methods to induce emotional fragility in a person they are targeting.

Highly sensitive people are those individuals who process information at a deeper level and are more aware of the subtleties in social dynamics. They have lots of positive attributes because they tend to be very considerate of others, and they watch their step to avoid causing people any harm, whether directly or indirectly. Such people tend to dislike any form of violence or cruelty, and they are easily upset by news reports about disastrous occurrences, or even depictions of gory scenes in movies.

Sensitive people also tend to get emotionally exhausted from taking in other people's feelings. When they walk into a room, they have the immediate ability to detect other people's moods, because they are naturally skilled at identifying and interpreting other people's body language cues, facial expressions, and tonal variations.

Manipulators like to target sensitive people because they are easy to manipulate. If you are sensitive to certain things, manipulators can use them against you. They will feign certain emotions to draw sensitive people in so that they can exploit them.

Sensitive people also tend to scare easily. They have a heightened "startle reflex," which means that they are more likely to show clear signs of fear or nervousness in potentially threatening situations. For example, sensitive people are more likely to jump up when someone sneaks up on them, even before they determine whether they are in any real danger. If you are a sensitive person, this trait can be very difficult to hide, and malicious people will be able to see it from a mile away.

Sensitive people also tend to be withdrawn. They are mostly introverts, and they like to keep to themselves because social stimulation can be emotionally draining for them. Manipulators who are looking to control others are more likely to target people who are introverted because that trait makes it easy to isolate potential victims.

Manipulators can also identify sensitive people by listening to how they talk. Sensitive people tend to be very proper; they never use vulgar language, and they tend to be very politically correct because they are trying to avoid offending anyone. They also tend to be polite, and they say please and thank you more often than others. Manipulators go after such people because they know that they are too polite to dismiss them right away; sensitive people will indulge anyone because they don't want to be rude, and that gives maliciously people a way in.

Emphatic people

Emphatic people are generally similar to highly sensitive people, except that they are more attuned to the feelings of others and the energy of the world around them. They tend to internalize other people's suffering to the point that it becomes their own. In fact, for some of them, it can be difficult to distinguish someone's discomfort from their own. Emphatic people make the best partners because they feel everything you feel. However, this makes them particularly easy to manipulate, which is why malicious people like to target them.

Malicious people can feign certain emotions, and convey those emotions to emphatic people, who will feel them as though they were real. That opens them up for exploitation. Emphatic people are the favorite targets of psychopathic conmen because they feel so deeply for others. A conman can make up stories about financial difficulties and swindle lots of money from emphatic people.

The problem with being emphatic is that because you have such strong emotions, you easily dismiss your own doubts about people because you would much rather offer help to a person who turns out to be a lair than deny help to a person who turns out to be telling the truth.

Emphatic people have a big-hearts, and they tend to be extremely generous, often to their own detriment. They are highly charitable, and they feel guilty when others around them suffer, even if it's not their fault and they can't do anything about it. Malicious people have a very easy time taking such people on guilt trips. They are the kind of people who would willingly fork over their life savings to help their friends get out of debt, even if it means they would be ruined financially.

Malicious people like to get into relationships with emphatic people because they are easy to take advantage of. Emphatic people try to avoid getting into intimate relationships in the first place because they know that it's easy for them to get engulfed in such relationships and to lose their identities in the process. However, manipulators will doggedly pursue them because they know that once they get it, they can guilt the emphatic person into doing anything they want.

Fear of loneliness

Many people are afraid of being alone, but this fear is more heightened in a small percentage of the population. This kind of fear can be truly paralyzing for those who experience it, and it can open them up to exploitation by malicious people. For example, there are many people who stay in dysfunctional relationships because they are afraid, they will never find someone else to love them if they break up with an abusive partner. Manipulators can identify this fear in a victim, and they'll often do everything they can to fuel it further to make sure that the person is crippled by it. People who are afraid of being alone can tolerate or even rationalize any kind of abuse.

The fear of being alone can be easy to spot in a potential victim. People with this kind of fear tend to exude some level of desperation at the beginning of relationships, and they can sometimes come across as clingy. While ordinary people may think of being clingy as a red flag, manipulative people will see it as an opportunity to exploit somebody. If you are attached to them, they'll use manipulative techniques to make you even more dependent on them. They can withhold love and affection (e.g., by using the silent treatment) to make the victim fear that he/she is about to get dumped so that they act out of desperation and cede more control to the manipulator.

The fear of being alone is, for the most part, a social construct, and it disproportionately affects women more than men. For generations, our society has taught women that their goal in life is to get married and have children, so, even the more progressive women who reject this social construct are still plagued by social pressures to adhere to those old standards. That being said, the fact is that men also tend to be afraid of being alone.

People with abandonment issues stemming from childhood tend to experience the fear of loneliness to a higher degree. There are also those people who may not necessarily fear loneliness in general, but they are afraid of being separated from the important people in their lives. For example, lots of people end up staying in abusive or dysfunctional relationships because they are afraid of being separated from their children.

Fear of disappointing others

We all feel a certain sense of obligation towards the people in our lives, but there are some people who are extremely afraid of disappointing others. This kind of fear is similar to the fear of embarrassment and the fear of rejection because it means that the person puts a lot of stock into how others perceive him or her. The fear of disappointing others can occur naturally, and it can actually be useful in some situations; parents who are afraid of disappointing their families will work harder to provide for them, and children who are afraid of disappointing their parents will study harder at school. In this case, the fear is actually constructive. However, it becomes unhealthy when it's directed at the wrong people, or when it forces you to compromise your own comfort and happiness.

When manipulators find out that you have a fear of disappointing others, they'll try to put you in a position where you feel like you owe them something. They'll do certain favors for you, and then they'll manipulate you into believing that you have a sense of obligation towards them. They will then guilt you into complying with any request whenever they want something from you.

Personality Dependent disorders and emotional dependency

Dependent personality disorder refers to a real disorder that is characterized by a person having an excessive and even pervasive need to be taken care of. This need often leads the person to be submissive towards the people in their lives and to be clingy and afraid of separation. People with this disorder act in ways that are meant to elicit caregiving. They tend to practice what's called "learned helplessness." This is where they act out of a conviction that they are unable to do certain things for themselves, and they need the help of others.

Such people have a hard time making decisions, even when dealing with simple things like picking out which clothes to wear. They need constant reassurance and advice, and they let others take the lead in their own lives. These are the kinds of people who either move back into their parents' homes as adults or treat their spouses and partners as though they are their parents.

Manipulators like to target people with dependent personality disorders because they are very easy to control and dominate. These people willingly cede control over their lives to others, so when manipulators come knocking, they don't face much resistance. Manipulators start off by giving them a false sense of security, but once they have won their trust, they switch gears and start imposing their will on them.

Emotional dependency is somewhat similar to dependent personality disorder, but it doesn't rise to the level of clinical significance. It stems from having low self-esteem, and it's often a result of childhood abandonment issues. People with an emotional dependency will play the submissive role in relationships for fear of losing their partners. They tend to be very agreeable because they want to please the people in their lives. Such people are easy to manipulate, and malicious people can easily dominate them.

Chapter 14. How to Identify and Counter A Manipulation

Identify it

The first key principle about manipulation can identify it. And to identify it, you have to understand the laws of human nature which are gotten from Robert Greene. The first law is that people will attack you if they think that you are weak. The second thing is that people are trying to sense any weakness in you to know whether they should attack you or back off. And the last one is that people are after easy victories. So, people are going to sense whether you are weak, and then they're going to think about whether they should attack you or not. If they feel like you're going to be an easy win, then they're going to attack you. And if they think that they are going to get hurt in the process, then they are going to back off and look for the easier victim. And the thing is that these people try to sense your weakness. If they sense that you are weak, they will attack you, and that is where you should use a defensive stand as an offensive stand.

So, to identify somebody who is a manipulator, you have to give up the impression that you are weak and that you are a naive person and that you depend on them because you want to see how they react to power. You want to see how they react when they feel like you have them. You want to appear like a weak victim and see how they react to it and see how they react to your weakness. Appear like you depend on them. Test them as much as you can. You want to appear weak to see how the person will react to you. Because that is when somebody really shows who they really are. So, to identify them, you, first of all, show that you're weak and see what happens. You want to test them; you don't want to get attached to them.

Build a reputation to avoid them

The following thing is to build a reputation to prevent manipulation. Your reputation is what precedes you in life. So, to determine manipulation, you must send signals that you are not to be messed around with. You have to send the signals, and you can do that by really taking bold actions. For instance, if you are with someone and you notice that they are starting to get too comfortable with you and they're starting to be late and get too comfortable, you can break it off. You can tell them that you are done, you don't like this kind of stuff with you, and that you have zero tolerance.

You are telling him that you could dump him any second if he messes around with you. If he's actually playing again, he's going to change that, and he will know that you are not somebody to be messed with. You want to set the tempo from the beginning. If you noticed that he's deviating from your standard and a healthy relationship, then cut him off.

If you see that he wants to act cool on you, then tell him that you are done. The thing is that you have to be willing to fish him out because that is the signal that people feel when you do that. They feel as if you can walk away any second. Most times, people are bluffing, and they show weakness. So, by actually making some bold moves like that, you are actually making them know that you know that they are playing games with you. So, in other words, you should make it like they got you all wrong because they thought that they are good by fucking with you, not knowing that they cannot mess around with you.

 Do the subtle thing that suggests that you are about to do it. This tells him that you are not paranoid. So if you're with somebody and you want to communicate with them that you're not happy with how things are going on and you're noticing that he is trying to guilt-trip and he's trying to make you do the things that he wants you to do rather, than say that you are going to leave him. Say subtle things that communicate that you are losing interest in him. For instance, not calling him back and telling him that you're not going to call him back or not calling him back when he texts you. So, you're responding in a very direct way, but you respond in a very bland way. The thoughts about you go away. There is no emotion when you text. There is no consistency when you text him. Don't stop till thing, and that will show him that you are losing interest in him. And that you are willing to walk away, and the guy knows that you are willing to walk away because of your past action.

Now since you are showing that you're losing interest, the guy will start changing his behavior. So, you must show people that you don't need them. You must make them know that you have more than you are paying and more than you have. So that if you lose them, you will still be ok. This will make them stop such things. If they feel that you are going to dump them, they will respect you more. The feeling that you are about to dump them or the feeling that you are losing interest because of their stupidity will make them respect you. And when they respect you, they will not play these games with you because they know that you're not to be fuck with.

It is important to let them know that if they mess with you, you will not be nice anymore, and you'll be downright difficult to deal with If the fuck with you.

You are going to communicate that you are not easy to deal with. So you have to be like that with yourself, or you have to realize that people are looking for an easy win and if you don't give them a hard time when they are looking for shit, they are going to keep giving you shit because it feels good to put all your problems into someone. So, one thing that you can do is that you should tell him a story of how somebody did the same shit and you dump them. You may say, "I remember one time that one dude kept fucking up with me, and I stop going out with him. I literally told him that we are done because he kept being late to the date, and I found it disrespectful". And he might say, "for real, you dumped him, and you will say yes if somebody messes with me, I will dump him." I am I like you a lot for one second, but if I feel that you are disrespecting me and you are playing games with me, then I will be done with the relationship".

Then you can just change the topic, and in his mind, he will know that you are no joke and that you're not a person to you fuck with. That's one way to do it. Tell them a story in the past of how you dump somebody that fucked with you.

Know how you feel around them

Now the best way to catch them is by knowing how you feel around them. So, you have to be aware of the way you are feeling around them. Usually, they make you feel discomfort around them. Also, they try to put you down. They make you hurt, and you find yourself thinking about what they said for a long time or finding out that they said some things that hurt you, even though you did not feel it during the conversation. Their behavior is recurrent, which means they try to do it repeatedly. They also push you to do things for them, and they only appreciate you when you do what they want.

They are moody about you. Today, you are the best person in the world; and the next day, they cannot believe that you exist in the world. What they really do is that they pretend to be on your side while they're working behind your back. They work behind your back subliminally, and they do that when they find out you are vulnerable. They don't hurt you directly, but they hurt you sublimely, and they do that to serve their real purpose. When you start to know them, they really become aggressive whenever they are confronted or whenever they're told that they are wrong. Whenever they feel that they will lose an argument or when they feel that you are winning the argument, they become very aggressive. You can also tell this kind of people through the words that they use, that they try to manipulate you.

They try to look really innocent and easy going with you. They tell you that they are not trying to put you down, but then they say something hurtful or negative to you. They start by putting you at ease and tell you that they are not trying to hurt you, that they really like you. Sometimes when you actually face them or confront them with what they are doing, they start telling that it is your fault. That what you did is making them act that way.

They even make you pity them by saying that they hate themselves because of how you make them feel or how you behave with them because you are not giving them all to supposed to give them. You should watch for any subtle statement or sarcasm that tries to put you down. These people are very dangerous when they are in contact with you, especially when they're your close friend, a boss, a co-worker, a wife, or a husband.

Run for your life

If you know someone like this, try to run for your Life stays away from this kind of Personality because they can do some psychological damage to you. Sometimes you may not be able to run away from this kind of person. You might start thinking about someone who will make you feel hot and uncomfortable, but you are not sure why. It is because they're manipulators. They are extremely smart. If they are in business, they are in a leadership position. And because they know how to manipulate and deceive others, they use it to get to what they need in your organization. Most people will actually have values, and they will trespass on the values just to get their own personal game. This type of person will do anything in their power, whether ethical or let go to get what you want. They are in your personal life and in your workplace. Them now, how do you deal with this kind of manipulative people.

Develop the right attitude

First, you have to develop the right attitude; you have to know that they are one of the most difficult people to deal with. So, you should remember that it is not your fault about the way they're behaving or a reaction to something bad that you have done even if they try to convince you that it is. Another thing you should remember is that you can never win the first square against them, so don't even do that because they don't even play fair, instead what they do need I to be able to maneuver you were around them and also had them.

Remember never to get absorbed by their drama, no matter how good they are. Do not allow them to find the stage for the fight because sometimes, they try to prepare, organize, and then set up a fight in a way to favor them. And also, do not trust anything that they say to you.

No matter what they say to you, they are sick. You should also have the right preparation and learn about their tactics. You need to learn about how they act around you. Try to expose them. Learn about them than about what they really are. Also, have social support around you that works which are people who support you and are positive around you. This will help to remove the effects of somebody who is Cunny and deceitful. If you can seek help from a supervisor from somebody, then seek help from somebody in authority or somebody who can help you and guide you whether it's a friend or your doctor. It is ok to seek help. It doesn't mean that you are wake.

Engage in physical activity

The next thing is to do a lot of activities that boost you morally, like sports. Sports are very good to help you feel good about yourself. Try to have routines, and disciplines that will help you build confidence in yourself, remember that it's not your fault you there, but that does not mean that you are a terrible person that or you are weak. Or that you are bad. If you feel that, then act. Just get up then from the scenario and trying to find smart ways to deal with that hurtful situation again. Most people fall into the trap of such personalities. Think about the right action.

Set the Rules of Engagement

One of the right actions to take is to set the Rules of Engagement. When you are dealing with such a person, make sure that you set the rules of engagement in your favor in a way that you will not get hurt. Do not allow them to drag you into their manipulation. Point out the inappropriate behavior. If they do something that does not make you feel comfortable, point it out, bring it up, and insist that they stop that abusive behavior. If they don't stop their behavior, then do not fight with them because you cannot win against them.

Refuse to engage in them refuse to tolerate that behavior tells them exactly what you want them to do or what you don't want them to do. You should remember that they can't be outsmarted. Most of them are spoilt kids. So, speak to their sick mind and tell them what it is for them. Prepare very well against them before having any engagement with them. Try to minimize engagement with them. Give them what they want, so that they will give you what you want. Do not give them anything free. Do not excuse their actions, no matter what they do will not excuse them. Even if what they are saying is relevant or true, know that it is he will put you down and able to manipulate you. They are not hurt by what you are doing. And feeling guilty.

They pretend to be hurt so that you will feel guilty, and they will control you. You will mostly see these people at work. And most people do not fit this description, but many people do. So, if you're confronted and have to deal with people like this, then you have to be able to trust your gut feeling. Sometimes we tell ourselves that we are doing something wrong because they are very good at manipulating you. So, you have to be able to protect yourself you need to have your own strategy on how to deal with them.

Do not be naive why most people are good at their Hearts. This kind of person is not good at the heart. Remember that not everybody will see their deception because they try to create that deception around you. So that you will doubt yourself they might not use, they are tricky on everybody at the same time. They chose their victims carefully. So do not assume that you'll be able to change them; nobody can change them. Even psychologists can fall into their trap occasionally.

Share your experiences

One way that you can do this, and help is to share your experiences. Most people are dealing with this kind of thing daily, and it is not easy to deal with. So, if you are sharing your experiences with other people, you be able to help other people with ideas, tips, and tricks that you have tried that worked, and things that try did not work.

Manipulation is a major problem even if it is only one person at work that it is doing all these things to you. They will turn your workplace into a very difficult, uncomfortable environment. Also, if you have this kind of person at home, they will turn your home environment into a very toxic, unhealthy environment. The world today has produced more of this kind of people than ever because of the corruption that is around us. We also have the same situation around the world because of the high mentality right now.

Almost Everybody now does things because of himself, and they don't care about whether other people are losing. If they are confronted with their problem, they will try to fight you, and they will never admit it. So, don't waste your time doing that. Instead, become the enemy, and when you become the enemy, you will be put under scrutiny and put you under their deceitful ways. They always find excuses not to believe you, or to even make it out yourself by saying that this is a waste of time what does this people know it is not me that has the problem it is you that has the problem. You should also try to pray and ask God for help always and it will help you get confident and overcome this kind of hurdles.

Chapter 15.Defending Yourself against Manipulation

Detecting Covert Manipulation

Covert manipulation, if you remember, is the manipulation of someone that is meant to be hidden. The person being manipulated should never be aware of the attempts happening. This is done through a series of actions that degrade self-esteem and self-confidence, which then leave the individual quite exposed and easily swayed. Learning to detect the following signs of covert manipulation will help you protect yourself in the future. If you learn the signs, you are far more likely to recognize them at the moment than someone who has little or no knowledge of manipulation.

Home court advantage

Those who are manipulative tend to seek control in any way they can get it, and they often see controlling the location for meetings or interactions as one of the easiest ways to get the advantage. Because the manipulator would then be able to dictate where a meeting occurs, they can be sure that they are fully comfortable with the interaction, whereas the other person, who is likely a target for manipulation, likely, is not comfortable. This means that a person will already be on edge, distracting from manipulation tactics that could be used.

Allowing you to speak first

By letting you speak, the manipulator is able to learn things about you to begin identifying how best to manipulate you. Think of the salesperson asking you what kind of car you are interested in. While you could answer with something simple, such as, "I want a truck with four doors," or listing the exact car you want, the salesperson tempts you into answering by asking what kind. You may answer that you are looking for a truck that can be used both to haul equipment for your job, but also has space in the back for car seats for your two children. Already, you have provided the manipulator with valuable information that can be used to sway you into a car that is more expensive than you likely would have initially wanted, and it is all because you were allowed to speak first.

Lying or manipulating facts or quotes

Oftentimes, manipulators will lie about facts. They may try to twist facts around to benefit themselves in hopes of keeping you just distracted or off-kilter enough that you do not notice or call them out on lying. They may misquote you just slightly in an attempt to use your words against you, or they may twist a phrase that someone influential used in order to ensure that whatever information is being presented is going to be beneficial to the manipulator. Think of the quote, "Blood is thicker than water." This is used as a way to say that you owe your loyalty to family, and that blood family is more important than anything else. However, this quote was initially, "Blood of the covenant is thicker than the water of the womb." The original meaning was meant to be that promises made, bonds forged through choice and oaths sworn, were far more important than blood relatives. This is what manipulators do with their own facts: they corrupt what was said into something that serves their own agendas.

Overwhelming you with statistics

Along with misquoting or even lying about things, manipulators also tend to throw enormous amounts of knowledge at someone in an attempt to make them appear more knowledgeable. They are able to do this particularly when the other person does not know as much about what is being explained. The manipulator seeks to be seen as an authority—as you should remember, one of the ways to persuade others is through appealing to authority, which is exactly what the manipulator seeks to do when inundating you with vast amounts of knowledge about a subject, even when a good portion of it is likely irrelevant to whatever you are discussing in the first place. Because you are likely to see someone spouting off vast amounts of useless knowledge about a subject as an authority on that particular topic, you are more likely to allow him or her to do whatever he or she is proposing solely due to your perception of that person as an authority figure.

Scapegoating laws or procedures

Particularly in office settings where there is plenty of bureaucracy, manipulators will seek to use this as reasons for certain decisions, or denials. They will use the rules that are on the paper in any way that benefits them, even going so far as to cherry-pick which policies and rules apply to them, but they will hold everyone else accountable. This can cause slowdowns on certain things, such as requesting time off or to use vacation hours—they may be allowed to act with discretion but choose not to solely to punish or manipulate others into doing their bidding. Those who are willing to follow the manipulator's leads may get that flexibility while everyone else is punished, so to speak, with regulations.

Raising voices or displaying displeasure

Though manipulators often think of themselves as emotionally intelligent and crafty, they are often the exact opposite. They struggle to control their own emotions, especially when emotions run high, and may inadvertently end up exploding in anger. They may also use louder voices and aggressive displays of displeasure in ways that will encourage people to give in out of intimidation rather than out of willingness. Through acting almost belligerently, they establish themselves as people to be feared, which typically give them a reputation of being intimidated. People are typically a lot less willing to argue with someone they know is a hothead, even if the declared hothead is wrong.

Negative or undesired surprises

Another common tactic within covert manipulation involves creating negative surprises or presenting someone with something unexpected in order to throw off people. For example, if you are going into a negotiation meeting believe that you and the other company have reached a settlement, the other side may instead lowball you when you show up to sign the paperwork. This is meant to knock you off guard, as you get so caught up in the unexpected, unrealistic suggestion that you may be distracted. Further, you have had little time to prepare a counteroffer, meaning that you are at a large disadvantage. They may then prey off of your unpreparedness, using it to say that they will need something more from you if you want to postpone negotiations again.

Withholding time

Manipulators will constrict available time, making time seem far scarier than it actually is in hopes of forcing you into making a decision that is not as well thought out as your decision might have been if you had slept on it. This is typical in sales positions in which you are signing a contract for a big-ticket item, such as a car or a house. The less time you have to debate your decision, the less informed you will be, and the less likely you are to think twice about it. If you are told you have until the end of the business day before a deal expires, for example, and you realize that it is 4:45 PM at that particular moment, you have fifteen minutes to make your decision before your deal expires. You may try to weigh the pros and cons, but ultimately, you will be more easily swayed at the moment than if you have time to think rationally, make pros/cons charts, or talk the decision through with your spouse to decide if it actually makes sense for you.

Sarcastic humor

This sort of humor is meant to chip away at your self-esteem. The worse your self-esteem gets, the more likely you are to be easily manipulated. Many manipulators will seek to create that low self-esteem through disparaging comments that are hidden behind jokes. They may make a comment about your last-generation phone, or that you never graduated from college, or even that you chose to eat beef during the work luncheon—after all, didn't you know that cows contribute to more greenhouse gasses than cars? Anything that draws attention to you or your choices in a way that downplays them or implies that they are bad choices are big wins for the manipulator, and if you dare get upset, the manipulator will laugh and declare it a joke. You are then left feeling inferior and uncomfortable in your decisions, doubting your judgment and your feelings. If you see someone disparaging others, constantly nit-picking at even the most irrelevant things, they may be a manipulator seeking to break their next target.

Judging and criticizing you or others

Along with sarcastic humor, but far less covert, manipulators have a tendency to judge others, and show no guilt about doing it verbally. They may always identify something that is wrong, but not denies it as a joke. They may look at your handwriting and declare it is nearly illegible or see a typo in your work and claim that you are unprofessional and lazy for not going back to read it. Even if you make it an effort to show up to work early in hopes of impressing this person, you may be told that you are too early and you should have taken the extra ten minutes to work on all of you, said with a demeaning hand wave at your entire self. Look for people that always have something negative to say to put people down but never provide any real criticism or advice on how to fix the problem—they are probably covert manipulators.

Playing dumb or incompetent

One of the most passive-aggressive marks of a covert manipulator is the attempt to feign ignorance. This is done in order to pretend he or she does not understand something or is unable to do it competently. Because they cannot do it, the burden of doing so then falls on someone else, enabling them to shirk off important duties. For example, imagine that your spouse always does the dishes wrong. You know that your spouse knows how to load a dishwasher—she lived by herself for years before the two of you got together, and the dishes were always immaculate when you went to visit. Now, however, it seems that she can never remember how to properly load the dishwasher and you always find dishes with food burnt onto them from the dry cycle, as well as large chunks of food stuck in the trap that should have been rinsed off. Dishes that are not supposed to be put in the dishwasher are, for some reason, and keep getting damaged or ruined. When you try to walk her through how to do the dishes, she nods like she understands, but never changes how she does them. This is an attempt to manipulate you into taking on the task of dishes because she does not want to do them.

Protecting Yourself from Manipulation Attempts

With an understanding of warning signs of covert manipulation, you are in a position to learn how to arm yourself against such manipulative actions. There are several tactics you can use in order to disarm a manipulator and escape exploitation. Seek to employ these different tactics to disempowering manipulators any time you start detecting signs of intentional manipulation attempts. You may find yourself becoming a far less desirable target if you put up any sort of fight.

Recognize your rights

Though this is important in a civil sense of knowing your constitutional rights as well, this is a reference to human rights. Human rights are the rights that every person is deserving of simply by virtue of being human. By recognizing your rights, you are able to protect them when you feel as though they are being infringed upon. Manipulation always infringes upon human rights, so knowing what your human rights are is the perfect way to judge this. Here are some of your most fundamental human rights, though there are others as well:

- You deserve to be regarded with respect. Every human should be treated with human decency.

- You are within your rights to express how you feel or what you want or think. This freedom to think means that you should be able to speak your mind without fear of repercussion.

- You control your priorities and goals. You have the right to decide what to pursue or what to avoid.

- You are within your rights to say no without guilt. You are not obligated to do anything you do not want to just because someone else tried to force it upon you.

- You have the right to protect yourself from physical, mental, or emotional harm. You deserve to be taken care of and physically, mentally, and emotionally whole and sound.

- You are within your rights to pursue a life that will bring you happiness.

These rights are typically going to be respected by most people, but manipulators do not care about them. The manipulators are thrilled to take away these rights in order to control you—in essence; you are nothing but an emotional slave to the manipulator. Ultimately, however, you are well within your rights to assert and enforce any of the above boundaries, as well as any other boundaries that make you comfortable, no matter how ridiculous other people may think they are.

Watch closely

One of the most surefire ways to avoid being manipulated is to avoid manipulators themselves. This involves studying other people and how they interact with the world around them. If you identify someone who is behaving in a way that you believe is likely manipulative, staying away from this person is a good way to avoid the hassle altogether.

When you engage in this sort of people-watching, look for extreme shifts in behaviors. While we all have ways that we tweak our behaviors depending on the context, typically, manipulators are within extremes. They are either polite or horribly rude. They may be aggressive to one person while gentle and kind to another, depending on the context. People who so drastically swing from one mood to the next depending on the person should be kept at an arm's distance.

Look for self-blame and counter it

Oftentimes, manipulators will instill self-blame and self-doubt within their targets. This is done by exploiting weaknesses and sensitivities. We all have moments of feeling like we are insufficient or unsatisfactory sometimes, however, if you notice that you begin to feel this way more frequently than usual, you should stop and seek to analyze why you are having those feelings. It may be time to reflect on whatever relationship you have with that particular person you associate with those feelings of inadequacy and determine whether the relationship is worth continuing. You may ask yourself if you are being respected within the relationship, or if current demands upon you are reasonable. The most important self-reflection, however, is that you should identify whether you feel good and comfortable within the relationship or if the relationship should continue.

Shift the focus

Instead of giving in to whatever the manipulator demands, try shifting the focus back to the manipulator instead of allowing it to remain on you. You could ask if the manipulator thinks the assertions or requests seem reasonable or ask if you are going to get something out of the current arrangement. Considering that most manipulators go out of their way to avoid blame or detection, by returning the focus of the conversation back to them, you make yourself seem far less attractive as a potential target. The manipulator may instead withdraw any attempts to sway you and move on to someone else.

Use time

Just as manipulators try to weaponized time, you too can use it to your advantage. Instead of pressing for a rushed decision, answer that you will consider it, but do not commit. You can remove yourself from the other person's manipulation attempt simply by taking the power back. With an assertion that you will think about it and answer later, there is no wiggle room for the manipulator to force your hand.

Say no—and mean it

Some people struggle to say no to others. Particularly those with lower self-esteem may really struggle with such a feat. However, by learning how to say no without justifying yourself or your reasoning, and enforcing that particular decision, you are able to remove power from manipulators. Manipulators prey on people's inability to say no, or the discomfort of displeasing people, so if you master the art of saying no, you are no longer an attractive target. If the manipulator does try to push past the no or disrespect your decision and boundary, you are well within your rights to set some sort of consequence as well. After all, sometimes the only way someone learns is through consequences.

Chapter 16. Manipulation in Relationships

A significant proportion of manipulation occurs in close relationships, especially romantic ones. In fact, manipulation of all forms in romantic relationships has become almost like a pandemic. Many people find themselves stuck in relationships where they are controlled by their partners. Some even find themselves being controlled by their children.

The peculiar thing about manipulative relationships is how they are toxic to all parties involved. The victim of manipulation loses all self-esteem and finds their individual identity shattered in the long run, while the manipulator finds it impossible to keep relationships with loved ones or maintain friendships with coworkers and acquaintances.

Manipulators in manipulative relationships can have very twisted motivations. Some, chiefly due to psychopathic tendencies, see manipulations as a merely gratifying activity. They manipulate others for recreation, almost as if it's a game. Some others are so fueled by a quest for power that they are ready to destroy the other individual(s) just to feel superior. They are control-happy domination freaks who like nothing other than to feel on top at all times. Some, as a result of their low self-esteem, manipulate others in their relationships because bringing someone else down helps them feel better about themselves, while others simply do so because they see no other way to advance their personal agendas.

One of the primary defenses against manipulation in relationships, just like manipulation in other circumstances, is awareness. Most times, you may not need to know what techniques your manipulators are using before knowing that you've been a victim of manipulation. You just need to look at yourself. Still, because of the strong ties you may have with your partner, you may feel some reluctance in ending a manipulative relationship even after deducing serious manipulative tendencies. This book can only go so far in helping you realize ways in which others may be trying with your mind or pulling at your puppet strings. It is up to you to determine if there is anything at all that's salvageable in the relationship. Experience has shown, though, that it is generally in the best interests of both parties to dissolve manipulative romantic relationships. If you realize that your partner or child or relative is manipulating you and you don't take concrete action, you're effectively enabling their poisonous behavior, which is neither good for them nor you.

Even if you're lucky enough to be in a healthy relationship that's characterized by love, understanding, and open communication, you may realize that you're wondering why some people stay in relationships that hurt them. Why would anyone continue a relationship with someone who makes them frustrated, self-doubting, scared, depressed, or confused? Why would anyone punish themselves so?

One thing you must understand is that most manipulative relationships don't begin that way. He/She may be so sweet at first, it's like they are an angel sent from heaven to illuminate your life. You have the perfect honeymoon, and everything is just amazing. Things go well for a bit, but then begin to turn sour. Because you have somehow been sold the idea by this manipulative partner that the downturn in the relationship is your fault, you blame yourself for the problems and persist, trying to regain your partner's love and loyalty for the wrong you have been made—through subtle techniques—to believe that you committed. Your efforts pay off and you and your partner are back together and in love again, but only for a while. Then the vicious cycle begins all over again.

Also, you must be aware that manipulation in relationships evolves over time. In almost all cases, it starts slowly, building up until it escalates. The abuser in this instance grows more confident in their manipulation tactics over time, entrapping the victim in a mental loop perpetuated by uncertainty and doubt, wherein the victim is controlled through a series of promised benefits and threatened repercussions, almost as if they are about to get what they desire but could have it taken away at any time.

Warning Signs of Manipulation in a Relationship

If you are in a relationship, especially a romantic one, and you observe any of these, there's a large chance that you're being manipulated.

1. You don't feel as good about yourself now as you did when the relationship began. You feel less in control of yourself, less sane, less intelligent, less confident, less secure, or even less attractive.

2. Your partner seems to arbitrarily withdraw their affection at the slightest provocation. So, you police your words, careful not to trigger them into absolute withdrawal because of what you say.

3. Just to make your partner happy and keep the relationship intact, you begin to do things that go against your values and beliefs. You're constantly in ethical dilemmas, and you find yourself crossing boundaries that you ordinarily wouldn't have crossed.

4. You know you're unhappy with the relationship and filled with uncertainty, but somehow you can't bring yourself to call it quits, mostly because the other person makes you blissfully happy on some occasions.

5. You were filled with joy when this person came into your life. Now, this joy has become sadness and desperation.

6. Your mood depends heavily on the general state of the relationship, and these days you've been going through drastic highs and severe lows simultaneously.

7. You talk about your relationship every time and to everyone who cares to listen. It doesn't dissipate the weight in your chest. You become an analyst, scrutinizing every detail in hopes that at a point, it'll all make sense to you. Pondering about the relationship so much makes you obsessive and paranoid.

8. You don't understand why, but your relationship seems bizarre and difficult to explain. Each time you try to lay it out to someone, you find yourself concluding that they may be unable to reason certain aspects because it's all "so complicated".

9. The best thing that ever happened to you is ruined and you feel strongly that you're responsible, though you don't know exactly what you did to mess it up.

10. You're always unsettled when your partner is not at home. You've developed an obsessive compulsion to know their exact whereabouts at any point in time because you don't have a clue

where they might exactly be. You become a stalker, policing your partner's social media account, emails, texts, and browser history.

11. You frequently ask the person you are in a relationship with if something is wrong and they tell you that everything is fine, but inside of you you're completely certain that something is amiss.

12. Your partner pulls away from you, and you blame yourself. You cannot understand why you keep sabotaging your relationship. You find yourself always apologizing and trying to repair the damage you believe you have caused.

13. You feel inadequate because regardless of your best efforts, you can't seem to make your partner happy. You used to be able to, but suddenly you lost the ability to bring a smile to their face. You cannot pinpoint the exact point where you began to get it wrong.

14. You find yourself feeling increasingly insecure, mistrustful, and filled with a strong fear of abandonment.

15. You always feel like you're falling short of your partner's expectations no matter what you do. This leads to you developing a problem with distrust, anger, insecurity, jealousy, and overreaction, which your partner points out to you from time to time.

If any of these is going on in your life, then you need to check yourself. Your partner is most likely manipulating you, and they may not even realize it. It is still up to you to decide on the next steps to take when manipulation his been diagnosed, but remember, under no circumstances will you ever have a social obligation to be victimized.

Categories of Manipulators in Relationships

One of the most dangerous things about manipulators in relationships is how they generally do not care about the extent of psychological damage they inflict on you with their actions, as long as they achieve the results to which they're aiming. They will try to play dumb and feign ignorance when you accuse them of something wrong that they have done, they hate your honesty, and they may brandish anger or abandonment to keep you in check.

It helps to know their techniques and have an idea of the warning signs, but to truly protect yourself from manipulation in relationships, it helps to go further into determining the kind of manipulator you're dealing with and how best to tackle them.

1. The Intimidator

It's very easy to be broken by someone you're afraid of. When you operate from a place of strength and self-assurance, however, you can put up a stronger fight and are better protected.

The intimidator is chiefly found in abusive spousal relationships where he or she reinforces aggressive fearmongering with violence. What the manipulator here does is strip away any sense of being able to defend yourself physically or psychologically, until you become putty in their hands. In such abusive relationships, anger is constantly used as a weapon, along with the threat of punishment, to instill significant fear in the victim.

2. The 'Pity Party'

This kind of manipulator is highly problematic because they are like a flu that keeps coming back over and over again. These 'pity party' manipulators twist the mind of their victims through guilt and sympathy, appealing to the natural sensibilities everyone has in which they feel the need to help others who are going through a rough patch.

Manipulators always look for ways to turn the sense of goodness that their victims have against them. They get into your head, painting such a pathetic scenario that your sense of charity is stirred. So, out of the kindness of your heart, you do what you can to help them out, meeting their every demand, and not realizing that you're being manipulated.

The worst part about 'pity party' manipulators is how their requests tend to increase in complexity and become more demanding, until they are practically issuing you commands while you shut yourself off from the world, focusing all your attention on trying to fix a thing that was never broken.

3. The Indifferent

This category of manipulators always acts like they don't care. No matter what you do, even when you have a significant cause for celebration, the indifferent manipulator acts like they wouldn't give a hoot if you vanished from the earth's surface and were never seen again.

This type of manipulation may seem apparent and easy to avoid, but not at all. By acting so indifferent, these individuals seize your attention. You begin to wonder about what you have done, second-guessing your own actions and trying to break through their shell. You spend time and energy trying to get their attention. Unbeknownst to you, they already singled you out. They will provide just enough interest to keep you hooked, but they won't break the cycle of indifference.

They make you become emotionally invested in them without as much a lifting a finger. At this point, they redirect your sympathy toward making them feel better with themselves.

4. The Critic

Manipulators in this category delight in destroying the confidence of their victims, especially when the victims seem to have an intrinsic need to please. They constantly criticize their victims, making them seem like they'll never be good enough, while simultaneously raising the bar of standards so high that the victim may never reach it. Through manipulation, critics make their victims feel worthless and establish that they are better than their victims.

This usually results in substantial personality changes, as the victim tries to be more like the critic, so they can feel better about themselves. The victim believes that if they walk and talk like the critic or develop the same preferences, they will develop a better sense of self-worth. This, however, is far from the truth, as they will only ever feel as good as the critic tells them that they are.

Tips for Handling Manipulation in Relationships

As has been established so far, manipulation in relationships is a serious ordeal that can severely damage both parties, but most especially the victim. Below are important techniques through which you can employ to resist manipulators in your relationships:

1. Call Manipulation Out for What It Is

One of the quickest ways to solve the problem is to label it for what it is. Labeling it shows that you have carefully identified the problem, which sets you on the track to deal with it. Many folks who are in manipulative relationships continue to wallow there because they do not want to acknowledge that they are being manipulated. Admitting that you're a victim of manipulation isn't a weakness; it's a strength.

You will never stop feeling like the problem if you don't admit to yourself that it was never really you, that you were simply a pawn in another person's game of chess. The longer you stay quiet about manipulation, the longer it goes on, and the more damage you incur. Remember, in a manipulative relationship, you are never the problem.

2. Don't Explain Yourself

One famous method of entrapment used by manipulators is making the victim feel like they have to explain their choices or rationalize their actions to them. The moment you recognize a manipulator in your relationship, instantly realize that you don't owe them any explanations.

It may be tempting but refrain from explaining to the manipulator why you need to take some time to think. They will act like it's their business, but you have to make them realize that it isn't. The moment you explain your need for space or, even worse, tell them what you intend to think about, you basically find yourself back in their clutches.

3. Give Yourself Some Time

Most manipulators are tactical. If you give them just a little space, they will fill up the entire room. When dealing with a manipulator, you need to take some time off. Manipulators will often make demands and expect instantaneous responses. Don't give it to them.

No matter how intensely they pressure you, stand your ground. You will only respond when you're ready after you've thought it all out properly. At the same time, never sound like you're asking for permission in any way, form, or shape, when you decide to take some time off. You don't want to put any power in their hands.

4. Remember That You Call the Shots

Never forget your right to the agency as an individual. When it comes to relationships, you have to be able to highlight your boundaries and stick with them. This will surely frustrate the manipulator, as they try to break through your boundaries, but you must stand your ground.

Set limits and be clear about them. If you do this, you will reclaim power over your life back from the manipulator.

Chapter 17. How to Deal with Psychopaths, Narcissists, and Chronically Manipulative People

Most of us use manipulation unknowingly and unconsciously once in a while to get what we want. In fact, you will find that everyone has used a mild manipulation tactic once a day, every day. Considering that something as simple as convincing your friend that you are fine when suffering is a way of manipulation, then we all have manipulative strengths.

However, there are maser manipulators- those people who strategically analyze how they will tune you until they get what they want. These people use manipulative techniques knowingly and consciously. They lookout for a vulnerable person, dig in their tentacles and then enjoy the ride.

There is another category of people who are chronically manipulative. Psychopaths are not just the villains you see in Wall Street morality scenes and slasher movies. They currently walk among us every day and appear like normal colleagues. In fact, one research revealed that a 3 to 4 percent of business leaders have a condition that meets the clinical definition of the term psychopath. That is a small figure, but very significant.

The same also applies for narcissists. Interestingly, researchers have found that a touch of narcissism in business can actually aid success. However, if you spend time in the work world, you will soon realize that some people let their self-love run wild.

The high and low of this is that in the course of normal life and career, you are 99 percent guaranteed to meet a few truly toxic psychopaths and narcissists who will try to manipulate and abuse you. That makes the difference between your success and failure.

You will be shocked to learn all the techniques that toxic manipulators can use to get to you. To mention a few, there is Gas-lighting, generalization, projection, changing of subjects, moving of goalposts, name-calling, devaluation, smear campaigns, triangulation, and aggressive jokes.

Gas-lighting

Gas-lighting, twisting facts and distorting information is common in the manipulation world.

Manipulators are known for messing the facts of any situation. They change it into whatever fits them. A manipulator using this technique will actually leave you confused and wondering if you had the facts right. In fact, the easiest way to define Gas-lighting is three phrases; 1) You imagined that 2) That did not happen 3) are you crazy?

Gas-lighting is probably one of the, most common yet toxic manipulation technique. It makes you doubt your sanity and knowledge and further erodes reality. Gradually, Gas-lighting eats away your ability to trust yourself. It inevitably disarms you and makes sure you feel afraid to call out mistreatment and abuse.

How can you defend yourself from Gas-lighting?

First, know your reality and have the facts right. You have to be sure about what you say in front of manipulative people. Do your research and have the supporting documents. Tell your friends what is happening so that they will remind you when needed. Ground yourself in reality.

Generalization

Supposing there is a project you are overseeing, and then you notice that there are some aspects (Maybe the financial segment) that might make it go south. You mention the same to a co-worker who then tells the manager that you said the project is a 'total disaster'. It is not that this person did not understand what you said- no. the fact is, he/she is not interested in what you have to say and is looking for ways to bring you down.

Maybe you talked about how a certain work colleague leaves out some important details when writing reports, the narcissistic co-worker will say that you said the colleague is a 'total failure'. The intention here is to make things sound worse than they really are then when called out, the narcissist will say that he/she did not understand.

Manipulative narcissists are intellectually lazy, therefore, instead of thinking on an individual level and taking everything in its own perspective, they will generalize everything under one term. They will put everything in one blanket statement leaving out the nuances in your arguments and taking out the unique perspectives you have identified.

To deal with this technique and people who use it, hold your truth. When you hear them distorting what you said, make a point of clarifying. Resist generalized statements and make sure that the narcissist understands the facts in his black and white understanding.

Projection

Surprise, we all use projection to protect ourselves once in a while. By definition, projection is what people do when they are claiming that all that negative energy is from that other person even if they know well it is theirs. Psychopaths and narcissistic people project nastiness on others a lot. They do this to displace responsibility for negative behavior by attributing it to someone else.

The counterattack of this is to not own projections. If someone accuses you of something you did not do, say it loud and clear that you did not have anything to do with whatever is going on. Also, do not project your negative energy onto others. If you do, you will be arming the manipulative person to return the favor, and believe me, it will not be nice.

Changing of subjects

Manipulative psychopaths and narcissists are also very good at changing the subject especially if the conversation is headed in a direction they do not like. This technique enables the victimizer to avoid taking responsibility. A manipulator does not want to be the topic; therefore, he/she will keep deflecting questions, especially if they become personal. They will reroute every subject in the way they see befitting them.

Manipulators can keep changing the subject for as long as you let them and will make hard to actually engage on relevant issues. For instance, if a boyfriend is cheating and the girlfriend confronts him/her about it, the boyfriend might start accusing her of being suspicious and untrusting. In the end, the couple will not sort the issue out.

The way to deal with this is acting like a broken record. Keep saying what you have to say even if the manipulative person tries to change the subject. Ignore all the distractions and focus on solving the issue at hand. Redirect him/her to the subject by saying "That is not what we are talking about. Let us address the real issue. If this person still is not interested in the real issues, disengage and spend your energy doing more constructive things. To make the manipulator realize that he/she is pushing you away, finish the conversation by saying "talk to me when you are ready to deal with the real issue."

Moving of goalposts

Manipulative Narcissist and psychopaths will always want you to feel intimidated so that they can have the upper hand on you. So, they do whatever it takes to make you feel invalid. In this line, these manipulators use a logical fallacy referred to as moving the goalposts whereby, anything you do will never meet their standards. Basically, these people set a standard and once you meet it, they add something to make it seem like you failed. They are perpetually unpleased with your work. You will have to keep proofing your abilities to them and they will never appreciate what you do.

The solution; Do not get trapped in that game. Remember you are not the problem. Constantly validate and approve yourself. Do not feel deficient or unworthy- that only empowers the manipulator to use you further.

Name-calling

Yes, there are adults who engage in name-calling, even p to presidential politics. And the truth is, just because we encountered name-calling since the first meeting with that bully does not mean that we will feel less affected by it. If anything, you are likely to feel more hurt today because you can process the insults on different levels and in a deeper way.

The only way to deal with this is do not tolerate it. If it is a conversation that is turning sour and name-calling starts, cut it off. Do not internalize negative things. Realize that the manipulator is using name-calling because he/she is not able to hold the conversation on a higher level, therefore, trying to pull you down.

Devaluation

Watch out for that colleague who is always saying negative things about the person who held your position before you came. That one is either a narcissist or a psychopath. Abusive manipulators don this all the time-degrading and devaluing another person, more so in his/her absence. Chances are, the manipulator will first make you feel important as if you are better than the other person then, he/she will start treating you badly.

The first step to countering this behavior is simply being aware of it. This will ensure that you detect the manipulator and take protective measures. Know that the way a person treats the ex might translate into the way you get treated in the future.

Triangulation

Triangulation involves reporting back falsehoods. The manipulator takes your attention away from his/her malicious intention by making you focus on another issue. He/she will make you pay attention to the supposed threat. Narcissists like to report what so and so said about so and so.

To counter this technique, realize that the supposed threat is also being manipulated. The manipulator is the real threat- that's who you should deal with. You can also try reverse triangulation whereby you report the manipulator to another manipulator and make them have an encounter.

Smear campaigns

When a toxic narcissist realizes that he/she cannot control you, he/she will try to control how others perceive you. A manipulator will take the role of the manipulator while you take the role of devil incarnate. If the people are being addressed do not know much about you, they will end up seeing you as the bad person. Technically, smear campaigns are designed to destroy your reputation and sabotage your name. Some of the pro manipulators will divide the crowd in two- for you and against you- and conquer.

However, do not fall for their trick. If you react to the statements made by such persons, it will signal them to continue. Remember that their intention is to hurt you and so long as they feel they are winning, that trend will continue. Do not over process what they say, instead, focus on what is important and act unbothered.

Aggressive jokes

Have you met those people who make nasty jokes then act as if it is it was nothing? In fact, they go ahead and tell you that your sense of humor needs revival? Well, the problem is not you or your sense of humor, rather, it is the manipulator who is actually being selfish. That offensive joke had some hidden intentions and that is why you feel cut. Covert manipulators like to make a malicious comment then hide behind the mask of "Just jokes" so that they can get away. They say appalling things and still try to look innocent, and cool. Whenever you get offended, they will claim that you are boring. Do not allow people to hurt you then claim it is just a joke.

How to outsmart a mastermind manipulator

A master manipulator is very good at what he/she does. He/she will make you turn to only him/her for comfort. The main difference between manipulators and other puppet masters is that they are very subtle. Further, master manipulators have only two goals; first, to get what they want and secondly, to never get caught. If they get caught, such information will spread very fast and victims will take cover. They sure do not want that. So, they tend to use their observation skills to analyses others and actively plan each step of their strategy. And anyone who has mastered manipulation will get away with it most of the time.

So, how can you outsmart manipulative people?

1.   Say no to manipulation

A large number of people feel sorry for others even when they do not deserve the pity. Consequently, they agree to things against their better judgment. If you find yourself in a situation where pitying a person will make you do things you would not do under normal circumstances, just say no. Turning people down might be hard at first, especially if you are used to helping everyone out but, that time has come to cut some of these people off. You are still good even if you say no. The more you think rationally, the easier it becomes to discern manipulation from genuine cases.

2.   Avoid contact with a manipulator

So, you have realized that a particular friend, relative, co-worker or whoever it is uses manipulative techniques to get what they want. What do you do? In the case of master manipulators, you better avoid contact. This person knows what he/she is doing and is aware of the consequences. If you confront him or her, be sure there will be an exchange and you might end up getting manipulated. It is better to stay away from this person. Now, doesn't that seem obvious? Yes, it does, but… easier said than done.

3.   Ignore the manipulator

Sometimes it can be hard to avoid some manipulators. For instance, if one is married to a manipulator, it might be hard to avoid him/her/. The best thing you can do in such a situation is ignoring the victimizer. Disregard their needs. Do not engage the, do not contradict them. Instead, listen to their owes, nod, then do whatever you wanted to do anyway. Do not let the lives of these manipulators be your undoing.

4.   Set boundaries

Personal boundaries are very important regardless of the relationship. Furthermore, boundaries are best set at the beginning of the relationship because then people do not know what to expect from you. For instance, if you show your classmates that your notes are easily available for them, they will keep asking for them

However, if you make it clear from the word go that your notes are personal property and can only be shared with people who missed class because of a really genuine and unavoidable reason, they will know better than to ask you. Let people know what you can and cannot tolerate in your life. If you are saying no, ensure there is a purpose. "No, you cannot use my notes because of A.B.C.D.". In some cases, you do not need to explain yourself. When dealing with some manipulative people who keep trying to overstep your boundaries even after you have made yourself clear, it is okay to be stubborn and a pain. After all, they too do not want to respect you.

## 5.	Set goals; they will help you notice when someone is trying to manipulate you

If you do not have standards and goals, chances are, a manipulator will have an easy time making you believe in anything g else. Define all your goals, professional career, personal improvement, relationships, and finances. The manipulator will then have a hard time making you get off your path. When you know your destination, it will be easy to notice when you are going off course. Detours and distractions become a lot clearer.

## 6.	Assume responsibility

Manipulators like to take credit for work they did not do. To deal with this such, make sure you assume responsibility for your actions, good, or bad.

A manipulator should not make you feel intimidated by blaming you for his/her mistakes. If he/she tries to pass you the blame, call him/her out. Knowing that you can stand for yourself will make the manipulator think twice before blaming you or claiming your work is theirs.

7.   Do not get involved emotionally

Reason and logic cannot be manipulated as much as emotions. If a master manipulator understands your emotions, and you let your emotional intelligence guard down, he or she will blow and twist your emotions to their liking. Soon enough you will feel out of sorts.

8.   Be the person people would rather avoid messing with

When setting boundaries, make sure that people know there are consequences. Make it risky for the manipulative person to get discovered. Let him/her know that it is hard to get things from you. Also, hit the manipulator where it hurts. For instance, if you discover that your boyfriend is cheating on you, let the other girls know he is A cheater.

Chapter 18.How to Learn to Use Manipulation to Your Advantage

A successful manipulator must have tactics at hand that will help them succeed at persuading people to achieve their own end goal. Although there are extreme theories that describe what a successful manipulator should be, we will consider three requirements defined by Georg K. Simon, a successful author in psychology.

Simon says that the manipulator will require to:

1. Hide their aggressive behaviors and intentions from the person or people they want to manipulate.

2. Determine the weaknesses of their intended subject or victims to identify the tactics that will be most ideal in achieving their goals.

3. Develop some degree of ruthlessness so that they will not handle any doubts that arise because of harming the subjects if it arrives at that. This harm can either be emotional or physical.

4. The motivating feature in manipulative interaction

Right now, you are aware that a significant characteristic of manipulative interaction is the realization that the "deliberate action" is the right choice for him in a certain situation. The ability of the manipulator to change the critical capacity to destroy the judgment may interfere with the awareness of the target, but it doesn't result in the change of direction.

This means that blurring and clouding affecting the critical capacity does not stimulate the "desirable" track. A strong incentive is needed to ensure that deliberate action is the first in the target's scale of choice. To realize this effect, the manipulator requires creating a link between the intentional action and the achievement of a powerful wish.

For the most part, the manipulator awakens a strong force in the subject's mind. He builds the notion that fulfillment can be attained if the target sticks to the instructions of the manipulator. The motivating factor in manipulative interaction shows a gap between the manipulator and the target. The target is trying to realize a powerful wish while the manipulator encourages him to do it by using incentives that create a false impression.

Manipulation as a motivating behavior

Manipulation is a motivating action. It is an effort by a person to make his or her colleague behave in a certain way, and for a certain purpose. The decision to manipulate and not apply a direct technique shows that the participants in the interaction have opposing stands. Robert Godin, in his book Manipulatory Politics, lists and criticizes a neo-Marxist view that describes the contradiction results from various interests. Manipulation basically works against the interest of those being manipulated. From this perspective, it is implicit that any encouraging action that is applied for the advantage of the target could never be part of the manipulation. This means the neo-Marxist view excludes the entire side of partially positive manipulations that are concentrated to progress the target's interests. Godin, who attempts to suggest an enhanced approach to the study of manipulative behavior, considers that the contradiction is facilitated by various wills and not essentially by contradicting interests, that is "One person—causing the other to act contrary to his putative will."

Godin's definition, which concentrates on contradictory wills, considers that the target's will, or at least his putative will, is always open to the manipulator. Usually enough, but, human beings like to speak in a different and contradictory voice simultaneously, which makes it difficult to understand what they really want. Does that imply that they cannot be manipulated?

Consider this, the rich housewife who keeps complaining that the maintenance task causes her to feel miserable, frustrated and unhappy, but she refuses to employ someone to help her. How could we forget to talk about the miserable Don Juan, who wants to get married, but constantly has love affairs only with married women? And perhaps there is the tragic example of the excellent musician who dedicated most of her life to learning the art of opera but keeps avoiding wonderful opportunities to audition in front of popular conductors who could be able to assist her to expand her professional career.

These three tragic heroes-the miserable housewives frustrated Don Juan, and the desperate musician is great examples that ambiguity regarding a person's intention will originate from the fact that he himself is confused and cannot make a decision. Ironically, manipulative interference can be useful in assisting the struggler to understand his will and arrive at a decision. Indeed, so many techniques in psychotherapy and education are designed to assist a confused person to discover his purpose and choose what to do with it.

The definition of Godin also appears problematic in scenarios where the manipulator and the target tend to share the same objectives. In those particular associations, the motivation to apply a manipulative approach can be pushed by different objectives on opportunities to complete the will, such as in the case where the target is in need to satisfy his will and realize his goals.

Now, we can look at Goodin's definition like an indirect move that is executed out of fear that a direct approach will face opposition.

But this preliminary broad definition demands a lot of care. In some cases, the decision to change depends wholly on efficiency where the manipulator tries to avoid long explanations and save time and effort. An extreme case is a leader who predicts a political crisis that demands a fast response. He assumes that describing the situation to his friends is a waste of time and decides to manipulate them instead.

Manipulation builds a free choice illusion

Manipulation is focused on changing the target to behave in a way that under normal conditions he resist.

However, most manipulative approaches are meant to cause the target to behave in a manner that is not in line with his intentions, interests, and motivations.

This property of manipulative behavior looks paradoxical. On the flipside, causing someone to act contrary to his priorities and preferences shows that manipulation has compelling aspects. On the other hand, the phrase manipulation itself, which is related to an elusive phenomenon like "maneuvering," shows that the target contains some judgment and consideration while he works. This tension can be corrected by including "illusory free choice," to the description of manipulative interaction.

Overall, the complex manipulator attempts to interfere, intrude and influence the decision-making process of the target by sending the impression that he selects the actions freely and independently. To accomplish this impact, the manipulator tries to make the target to see the "intentional action" as the best available choice in the present situation. The practical definition is that the target, who is subject to a hidden effect, believes that his choices are made independently and freely.

Hiding important information in order to attain the desired decision demonstrates the concept of "illusory free choice" in a manipulative interaction. The target, who knows that he selects the best available option freely and independently, is prone to invisible interference in his critical thinking and judgment.

Unfortunately, it is not hard to imagine opposite scenarios where an individual is convinced that he is on the correct track, making the best decision and not ready to consider other choices. Ironically, assisting him to understand the value of other possibilities demands the application of the unconventional methods of influence that specific manipulative strategies can deliver.

In the most difficult situations, the individual is held up in a biased conception of reality that is not ready to assess critically. There are various classic examples: the ambiguous young gentleman who is ready to become a great musician although he doesn't have any sense of rhythm; the courageous general who doesn't want to accept the fact that the enemy is going to attack, the diligent manufacturer who spend most of his money, effort, and time improving the quality of goods that are not in demand.

Instances of tragic entrenchment are costly because they limit the world perception of the trapped individual, destroy his adaptation to the continually changing instances of reality, and cause him and his environment a lot of misery and suffering. The relevant point is that a complex manipulative process can sometimes be the only hope in this case. An indirect approach of influence can convince the entrenched target to think twice on the validity of his biased stand.

In the following case, the manipulator can assist the entrenched target to look for other alternatives that he previously was not even ready to acknowledge. Paradoxically, in the initial stand, the target was aware that he was selecting the best available choice, while it is the manipulative interference that allowed him to make a real choice.

This strategy can be described as "liberation by manipulation." Briefly, this approach requires methods of influence in psychotherapy and education that are meant to develop the impression that the target is doing the change by himself. He is not supposed to realize that someone else is triggering the situation and assisting him to identify the path to change and improvement.

Manipulation is hidden from the target

Motivating by applying manipulative approaches intends to restrict any possibility of the target objecting to the manipulator's moves. The manipulator tries to prevent the target from considering specific operational possibilities or, alternatively, the manipulator tries to cause the target to factor possible actions that he refuses to assess. The manipulator tries to realize the motivating effect smoothly and elegantly. He wishes to build the impression that the target is selecting his actions freely and independently.

This effect could be accomplished because the process of manipulative interaction, the manipulator's field of vision is broader than the target. In other words, the manipulator tends to know a lot than the target. This means the manipulator can use the point of view of the target without the target being aware.

However, the ability of the target to learn about the manipulator's real intention provides him with the chance to consider other options apart from the goal of the manipulator.

This is exactly what the manipulator wants to prevent, otherwise, she would not move forward with the manipulation. The practical meaning is that the purpose has been exposed and the target can choose whether to surrender or refuse to cooperate based on the manipulator's instructions. So, it's not a matter of "illusory free choice" but real free choice. For that reason, the manipulative act fails or does not exist.

Based on the characterization, statements such as "you are manipulating me" are self-contradictions. It is not possible to become a victim of manipulation and, at the same time be aware of it. Additionally, it is likely that this confronting method was applied in order to change roles in the interaction. One way is that by leveling the accusation, you are trying to discover your hidden intentions.

Another way is to consider the statement "you are manipulating me" as an indirect message. In this case, "I am surrendering, but you have to know that you owe me." In a situation where the manipulator fails to see it, he gets exposed to the possibility of a future pressure without knowing it. The manipulator's focus of vision is smaller than the target's, and the practical meaning is that the initial manipulator fell in his own trap and became a victim of manipulation.

Manipulation changes the critical capacity

Critical capacity is a relevant mechanism that allows us to choose our actions based on our preferences and priorities. It is supposed to work like a dedicated guard whose responsibility is to maintain our decisions and behavior consistent with our self-interest and world perspective.

An encouraging action meant to direct a person to behave in contradiction to his choices without realizing the distortion must interfere, or at least avoid the inspection procedure. Manipulative action aims to affect the target's critical capacity. There are two strategies that are intended to achieve this:

The first one is obvious. The manipulator applies morally questionable approaches during the interaction to prevent any likely objection to his moves by the target. However, changing critical capacity can be applied to the advantage of the manipulator and it could be applied to enhance the target's stand.

The first example markets Erich Fromm's description of manipulative techniques applied by modern advertising to counteract critical judgment and encourage the selling of useless, or irrelevant goods. According to Fromm's description, a wide sector of modern advertising does not appeal to reason but to emotion.

The second example is derived from the field of psychotherapy. Milton Erickson's confusing style is meant to confuse the target. The concept is to destroy the target's critical capacity and make him work in a direction different from his intentions and priorities.

Overall, Erickson created and used the confusion technique for hypnosis. Later, he and colleagues applied the same technique in psychotherapy to confuse patients for a relevant change. The confusion decreases the patient's critical judgment and destroys his normal resistance to changing traditional habits that make him so much suffering. By reducing the target's critical awareness, Erickson expected to pave ways to discover new methods.

The second approach is meant to enhance and improve the target's critical capacity. But we should not forget that changing critical capacity is also a manipulative process. The final result of manipulation is to make the target to behave in a way that he would otherwise refuse. We have an important reason to doubt that the sophisticated manipulator only wants to develop the impression of assisting the target to develop and explain his critical capacity. The real intention is quite different.

The next example involves a manipulative workshop for creating critical capacity. A matchmaker is selected to choose a perfect bride for a young Jew. The young man who commits most of his time to study the bible has never dated a lady in his lifetime. As a great student, he learns from his mentor that the value of the bride is determined based on the status of her family. "The secret to a great marriage is that the bride comes from a good family," says the matchmaker.

Armed with this knowledge, our young hero goes for the first date to meet an unattractive, spoiled lady whose wealthy father "accidentally" paid the matchmaker a lot of money.

Funny stories involving manipulative strategies in traditional societies resemble tough approaches to sales promotion in modern times. Most of the time we need to purchase a device whose functions we don't understand, and we don't know how to compare several products. We step into the shop, and an elegant salesman is ready to assist. Tiny cases involve those where the manipulator has a great estimation of the target's preference. However, the potential to change critical capacity does not require this awareness. For instance, it can be effective to apply psychological knowledge and mathematical expertise to trigger the decision of a person. A popular technique is to develop a decision-making problem in a manner that would damage any possible objection to the manipulator's desired result. The choice of an individual can be reversed by defining a particular choice problem separately. If it is delivered as a choice between gains, one will probably go for the less risky option. But if it is delivered as a choice between losses, then one will go for the riskier option.

In general, the manipulator affects the target's decision by making him believe that he decides the best available option in a particular case. The target's understanding or misunderstanding of the situation shows that his critical capacity is paralyzed. In the following case, the manipulator can realize this effect by different means, rational arguments, temptation, and so on. The key point here is that manipulative behavior, as good as it may be, focuses to diminish the target's potential to judge critically the moves of the manipulator.

Chapter 19.Manipulation Tips and Tricks

The first tip in manipulation is the change of environment.

More often than not, your environment can influence how people react and respond to what you're asking for. For example, if you are in the workplace or any other kind of business environment, people in that environment with you will most likely see you as a rival or as a competitor. This would make it difficult for them to give in to your request. So, if you want to get people to agree to what you're requesting for, especially your work colleagues, take them out for a drink or a lunch date. The drinking environment or the lunch environment helps them see you less as a colleague and more as a friend, and everyone easily agrees to what your friend is asking for, right?

The second tip you can try out when manipulating people is to make it all about the person you want to manipulate.

Yes, your aim is to learn manipulation techniques to use on people for your own good. However, nobody would like to answer your request if they find out you are doing it for your own good. This means you have to be as subtle as possible, make your request all about the other person. How do you do this? When you render help to people, people will be willing to help you. So, if you want to manipulate someone, help the person out first, then they would be willing to help when you need it.

Another tip is to speak quickly.

Many great manipulators use this. The secret behind this is that when you speak very fast, people will find it difficult to understand what you're saying and when they don't know what you're saying, they will easily agree to what you're asking for.

How do you do this? Walk up briskly to someone that you want to manipulate, issue fast instructions, and leave immediately. This would not allow the person enough time to think upon what you said or react to what you said. Therefore, they would carry out your instructions even without understanding them. This especially works if you are in a position of authority. It will make your victim see you as an important person, and they will see you as someone who does not have the time to explain every detail. You can use this technique in car sales and various forms of business closing.

This following tip goes without saying, you have to dress nicely.

Before I knew how powerful this was in manipulating people, I could care less about how I looked or dressed. However, when I saw that this was a powerful manipulation tip, I began to literally dress to kill. Remember the aim of manipulation is to get your own good, so spend money on clothing, read books and magazines on how to look good and well-groomed, spend well on jewelry, a nice wristwatch and buy expensive perfumes. Try this for the following week can see how people react to you.

You see that when people complain about what happened to them when they encountered a con artist, one thing many of them say is that the con artist looked responsible, so they fell for him or her. The dressing goes a long way in helping you manipulate people.

So, research on what people term as good dressing in your location, spend well on it and go-ahead to talk to people you will see how easily they will give into your requests. Who doesn't like a person that looks good and smells good?

This following tip means you're going to be tapping into the basic survival instinct of every human being. It's called the scare tactics.

When I tell you that you have a lot to lose if you don't do what I want you to do, I am basically using scare tactics to manipulate you. That means if you want to manipulate someone using scare tactics, all you have to do is mention what the person might lose if the person doesn't do what you are asking for. Don't make it sound like a threat, just subtly do it.

When marketers or advertisers mention things like 'buy now', 'this offer will close in 3 days', 'get this now so that you'll be among the first ten people to get it' and so on, what these marketers do in such instances is to manipulate their listeners or potential buyers into getting what they want using scare tactics.

In scare tactics, you are tapping into the basic need to survive the unknown that all human beings have. This is what the insurance business uses. I come to you and tell you to pay an amount of money to protect yourself from unforeseen accidents that might happen in the future. All I just did was to scare you with what might happen. Since this has been proven to work in the insurance industry, you can also use it as a master manipulator. This is best used when you are manipulating someone to accept a solution that you want to give the person. Also, you can use it in relationships such as your work or personal relationships, you just have to get the right angle.

This following tip applies to every aspect of life. When you are consistent with something, you get results from it. So, if you're consistent with manipulation, you get results from it and get better at it. Now, how can you apply consistency to manipulation? This is easy, just stay in character. When you are acting like a nice person, be nice to everybody, the waiter, your work colleague, everybody. This will prevent people from seeing you as two different persons.

A master manipulator needs to be believed; people need to believe you. Now, if they need to believe you, you also need to stay faithful to the character you are trying to portray. Once they see a red flag in your character, once they see something conflicting in your character, they would notice it and not give in to your demands. Therefore, you need to be consistent in the way you speak and act to everybody. Speak in the same tone and manner to everybody, and that way you will easily win people over. This is especially true because a consistent person is seen as a person of integrity, and a person of integrity is easily believed. When they believe and trust you, you have them as putty in your palms.

This following tip is very easy to do. Why? This is because all you have to do is to keep quiet, silence is Golden. When you are silent around people, they get uncomfortable and their discomfort makes them give out information. How do you do this? Simple, just repeat the last two or three words of every statement that they make.

Let me show you an example:

Victim: I saw John in the morning.

Manipulator: John

Victim: Yes, John, I saw him at the phone store.

Manipulator: Phone store?

Victim: Yes, I went to buy a new phone for my daughter for her birthday.

Did you see what just happened now? The manipulator was able to get information from the victim by just keeping silent and asking just enough questions.

Wisdom, however, is not to do this too much. Else, you will begin to look awkward.

In this following tip, you would realize that it pays to be nice.

When you want to get someone to do what you want to do, you have to be as nice as possible even when internally, you are very angry. The reason for this is that people want to see how far you can go in staying nice, people want to see your breaking point. Therefore, you have to be positive always, begin your conversations on a happy note, stay in a happy tone, and with a positive note even when internally, you are angry, stay cool. Never let your anger show to the surface, rather, play nice.

The choice of words is very important in playing nice. You have to look at how best to say what you are about to say. Rather than make someone feel foolish with your words, you can make someone feel responsible and want to do the correct thing just by saying the right words. For example, you can say, "have you considered this option", rather than saying, "you must do this option."

In manipulation, nice words always work.

So far, it seems I'm showing you tips on how to live as a good human being right? Well, you're not too far from the truth, human beings are born to be natural manipulators. However, as we grow older, we begin to conform to society's rules, whims and caprices. This makes us forget our natural manipulative tendencies.

In this following tip, what I am going to tell you is that you should basically be responsible. Own up to your actions. Carry your cross!

When you do some things, people will easily think that you are a good person, someone that they should trust. For example, when a Christian or a person wears a rosary or a cross necklace on his neck or her neck, people would easily think that you are a person with good morals or a Christian. Once they believe this about you, they lower their defenses and attack instincts around you, and when they do this, you will find it easy to get them to do what you want.

So, what this means is that the accessories and items you carry along with you make you more agreeable to manipulate people. For example, if you are a man and you walk around with a cute dog, women would easily be attracted to you. This increases your appeal to women. Also, if you carry around a baby or your child, it will make you come up as a responsible man, and people would want to talk to you. Women would easily want to give you their numbers, you can even ask them out on a date, and they would agree.

Of course, for this tip, you don't need to carry or force a child to come along with you or even borrow your nephews and nieces. What you are trying to achieve here is creating an illusion or picturing yourself in the mind of the person you want to manipulate as someone that is responsible.

In this following trick, I am going to be showing you how to get people to believe what you are trying to portray about yourself. You are going to learn how to talk the talk and walk the walk. For example, if you sound stupid, everyone will assume that you are stupid. However, when you sound smart, people around you are shame you're smart and therefore take you seriously.

So rather than use filler words and sound like a teenage girl that no one would want to take seriously, you can broaden your vocabulary by listening to authorities in various fields and industries, great speakers and read a lot of books. Also, you can listen to the news as well as watch various documentaries on a wide range of subjects. This would make you have a big bank of things to say to make you sound intelligent.

Also, learn to measure your intellect. People like to trust people that sound intelligent. When you sound intelligent, they would easily give in to what you want them to think and believe this will make it easy for people to agree to your terms.

For this following tip, all you need to do is to be a good storyteller. People are more agreeable to a good storyteller. Great manipulators are great storytellers. Of course, there are times where you might need to back up what you say with data, but more often than not, a good storyteller always has the ear of his or her listeners.

Therefore, you need to put the data aside sometimes and tell stories. In your stories, use anecdotes, they make the story more personal and more human. If you don't have any personal anecdotes, you could always borrow from someone's story somewhere, just be creative.

The number one rule for manipulation is that you should stand out in the mind of the person you want to manipulate; they should remember you but not suspect you. For you to achieve this, you should use terms people use every day, be easy-going, talk about topics that just anybody talks about, the aim is for you to be predictable in a way that people can relate.

Therefore, you need to learn how to blend with the crowd. This would help you receive protection from the crowd around you. So, you don't need to forcibly be unique. Rather, be predictable and still sound smart and charming.

For this following trick or tip, you can decide to help the newbie in your company. Everybody trusts the person who wants to help. So, if you want to manipulate a newcomer in your company or environment, just render him or her some help. This will make them trust you and then give in easily to your demands. Once they give in to your demands, you can manipulate them as you like.

The statement 'I need your help' when crafted in some ways can either help you achieve your manipulative goals or reduce your hopes of achieving your manipulative goals. For example, if you are the boss of a company and yew bark out orders to your staff, of course, they would go-ahead to do what you want because they do not want to get fired. But when you give the same instructions and say them as 'I need your help', you're getting your staff to put in more to help you achieve what you want. This is the best because they do not just see you as their boss, they now see you as their colleague, just with a better office. Politicians do this a lot. They sit and eat with you so as to make you think that they are just one of your friends or neighbors who wants to make the community a better place. They do this for four years or five years and then cart away with the society's funds. So, you too can use this powerful trick to get people to do your whims and caprices.

One tip that works every time is food. It is a known fact that people are more agreeable when they have eaten. So, to win over the person you intend manipulating, ensure he or she is well fed. This would help them easily give in to what you want. A lot of business deals and contracts have been closed over dinners, there is a reason for this. You can try it out too.

So, which one out of these tips and tricks would you try out first? For me, I would definitely recommend starting with dressing and smelling good. This would go so well with offering help and looking responsible. Combining this would make you a master manipulator anytime.

Conclusion

You will agree with the assessment that manipulation is everywhere in our daily lives. Even while you sleep, there is a brand somewhere that is looking to unleash their manipulative marketing campaign with the goal of making you spend your money. While you slave away at work at the mercy of your boss, there is often no guarantee that you will get a promotion. In your personal relationships, there is probably someone who is pretending to be your friend but is only looking out for themselves. It almost seems like whichever way you turn, there is someone waiting to influence your next move. This can be quite overwhelming.

Being manipulated does not feel good. Knowing that everything you thought was true was an altered reality created by a manipulative person makes you feel betrayed and, often times, stupid. You wonder why you did not see the red flags and what you could have done differently. The truth of the matter is that however smart you think you are, there is always someone who believes they can outsmart you. Enter your new manipulation methods.

You do not have to sit back and watch other people take control and get what you want when you can do it yourself. Influencing other people into fulfilling your desires is well within your reach if you internalize and incorporate the teachings and methods of this book. It might seem like an uphill climb, especially if you are used to giving other people what they want and getting nothing in return, but it really is not. Learning how to manipulate people is not something that should overwhelm you. It only feels overwhelming now because you are learning all these new things all at once. With time and practice, the things you have learned will become second nature. You will find yourself smiling and flirting without even thinking about it.